Ancient Peoples and Places

THE MEDES
AND PERSIANS

General Editor

DR. GLYN DANIEL

ABOUT THE AUTHOR

William Culican was educated at Preston Catholic College and the Universities of Edinburgh and Oxford. He has travelled widely in the countries of the Mediterranean and the Near East in connection with his special fields of study, ancient Persia and Phoenicia.

In 1957 Mr. Culican was Tweedie Exploration Fellow of the University of Edinburgh and in 1958 held a Treasury Scholarship for the study of Akkadian. He is now Senior Lecturer in Semitic Studies at the University of Melbourne, as well as honorary curator of Near Eastern Art in the National Gallery of Victoria.

A contributor to various learned journals, Mr. Culican is assistant editor to two journals concerned with Semitic Studies and Near Eastern Religion.

Ancient Peoples and Places

THE MEDES
AND PERSIANS

William Culican

76 PHOTOGRAPHS
52 LINE DRAWINGS
2 MAPS
2 TABLES

FREDERICK A. PRAEGER
Publishers
New York · Washington

THIS IS VOLUME FORTY-TWO IN THE SERIES
Ancient Peoples and Places
GENERAL EDITOR: DR. GLYN DANIEL

BOOKS THAT MATTER

*Published in the United States of America
in 1965 by Frederick A. Praeger, Inc.
Publishers, 111 Fourth Avenue
New York 3, N.Y.*
© *William Culican 1965*
Library of Congress Catalog Card Number: 65-16727
Printed in Great Britain

CONTENTS

ILLUSTRATIONS

8

Bracketed numbers *after the captions* refer to works in the Bibliography.

10

Preface

They say the Lion and the Lizard keep
The Courts where Jamshyd gloried and drank deep:
And Bahram, that great Hunter – the Wild Ass
Stamps o'er his Head, and he lies fast asleep.

E. Fitzgerald: OMAR KHAYYÁM

No RUINS of oriental antiquity had so great an impact on the Western world as those of the palace of Persepolis. Begun by Darius about 518 BC, it was completed by Xerxes. It stood in a mountain valley of south-western Iran, in the homeland of the Achaemenid clan, and was the first great monument of Empire the world had known. In it each New Year's day the Achaemenid kingship was renewed and men from every part of the empire came to offer their tokens of obeisance. Here Darius planned to invade both India and Europe; here Xerxes plotted the war with Greece. Long after it had been burnt down by Alexander the Great, its massive 65 foot columns and staircases stood as a reminder. Legends were woven about the ruins. It was known as Takht-i Jamshyd, the throne of the prehistoric legendary Iranian hero Jamshyd, where he 'gloried and drank deep'.

In the Middle Ages, travellers like the monk Oderic of Pordenone (1320), Giosafat Barbaro (1474), the Englishmen Geoffrey Duckett (1520) and Thomas Herbert (1628), and the German von Poser (1621) all saw and admired the ruins. More significantly, it was from these ruins that the Venetian consul Pietro della Valle brought back to Venice about 1622 the first cuneiform inscription known in the West. Although two centuries were to elapse before any real advance in the decipherment of this mysterious script, here was a challenge that whetted the appetite of scholars and began a long if spasmodic attempt to understand. In 1765 the Danish scholar Karsten Niebuhr made careful copies of the Persepolis inscriptions and published them. These were soon recognised as trilingual and in 1802, aided by his knowledge of surviving old Persian in the Avesta and in Parsee literature, Grotefend of Germany succeeded in producing an extensive translation of an Achaemenid cuneiform inscription. There followed Henry Rawlinson's translation of the Old Persian columns of the rock inscription of Darius I at Behistun, and in 1851, only a few years after the beginning of excavations by Botta and Layard at Nimrud, Khorsabad and Nineveh, came his translation of the Akkadian version of the same inscription. Thus through the Old Persian of Persepolis the system of cuneiform script was deciphered. In Persepolis the key to the secrets of ancient West Asiatic civilisation had lain hidden.

It was della Valle who first identified the ruins as Takht-i Jamshyd: he knew nothing of its true history, since Persepolis had made little impact on classical authors. But by 1625, as shown in the charming etchings of the Dutchman Philip Angel, the ruins were recognised as 'Old Persepolis'. His remarkably accurate drawings mark the remote beginning of field archaeology in Iran.

Very few books have been written about the Medes and Achaemenids. Their history is complex and limitations of time and place cannot conveniently be imposed upon them. The personalities and activities of their kings are less documented in many ways than those of the kings of Assyria and Babylon, and all historians must fall back on Herodotus and Thucydides for much of their material. In writing this book for an archaeological series, I have compressed the historical aspect and concentrated mainly on art-history and the interpretation of documents, since these are our only hope of fresh information. In the first two chapters I have aimed to present those aspects of Iranian archaeology which seemed significant in the genesis of the culture of the Medes and Persians.

In the writing of this book I owe a special debt to the Baillieu Library of the University of Melbourne for generous patience over obtaining microfilms of articles not available in Australia, to the National Gallery of Victoria and the Australian Institute of Archaeology for library facilities, to my wife and Miss E. Marso for reading and emending the text, and to various collectors who have permitted me to reproduce draw, ings of materials in their private possession.

I am grateful for permission to reproduce items in the fol, lowing museums: Metropolitan Museum, New York; The British Museum; the Louvre, Paris; The Hermitage Museum, Leningrad; Cincinnati Art Museum; Museum of Fine Arts, Boston; Nelson Museum – Atkins Gallery, Kansas City; The Brooklyn Museum; Institute of Arts, Minneapolis; Cleveland Museum of Art; City Art Museum, St Louis; Seattle Art Museum; also Messrs Bulloz, Dräyer, Giraudon, Perissinotto and Miss J. Powell for photographs of Persepolis and of objects in the Teheran Archaeological Museum as well as in private collections shown in the various exhibitions '7000 Years of Art in Iran'. I wish to record my thanks to Mr and Mrs Alastair Bradley Martin for Plate 60 and to Mr Khalil Rabenou for permission to include Figure 10a. I am indebted to J. Menant's *La glyptique orientale* for Figure 54; E. J. Brill publishers for Figure 9; and *Berliner Museen*; *Berichte aus den Preussischen Kunstsammlungen*, 1934, for Plate 71.

Finally, I wish to thank Mr H. A. Shelley for drawing the maps (Figs. 16, 23) from my own rough sketches, Mr Jon Wilsher for redrawing the Susa column capital (Fig. 24) and Mr Gerard Bakker for making the simplified plan of the Persepolis palace (Fig. 26).

W.C.

IRANIANS IN THE FIRST MILLENNIUM BC

1100–1000	New settlements of Aryans, users of black polished pottery, in north and west Iran
900 onwards	Growth of Urartian kingdom around Lake Van
835	King Shalmaneser III of Assyria receives homage from 27 kings of Parsua-land (west of Lake Urmiya) and enters Mada-land (Upper Zagros)
c. 829	Urartu wins control of Mannai and Mada from Shamsi-Adad V, who encounters chieftains with specifically Iranian names
812–782	Adadnirari III claims subjection of Madai and Parsua
c. 730	Tiglathpileser III encounters Parsua folk in central Zagros
719	Sargon II establishes central *Parsuash* (Kirmansah) as an Assyrian province
715	Daiaukku (Herodotus' Deioces), a Mannaean or Median chieftain, joins Urartu in an anti-Assyrian alliance. He is captured by Sargon and exiled
712	Ukshatar (Cyaxares I), a rebellious chieftain of north Zagros, pays tribute to Sargon
710 onwards	Medes form extensive kingdom in north Iran

700–650	Pursua folk move south into Parsumash (Bakhtiari hills): 692, Sennacherib lists Anshan and Parsumash amongst his foes
700–668	Cimmerian invasion. Mannai revolt joined by Ishpakaia, a Scythian
678	Teushpa, a Cimmerian leader, breaks Assyrian hold on Kurdistan
675?	Teispes (Chishpish), son of Hakamanish of Parsumash, takes Anshan
674	Kashtaritu⁄Khshathrita (Phraortes son of Deioces?) leads a coalition of Medes, Mannai and Cimmerians against Esarhaddon
670	Khshathrita takes Parsumash, reduces Teispes to vassalage
660	Assurbanipal regains Mannaean territory
653?	Khshathrita dies, eventually succeeded by his son Khuvakh⁄shatra (Cyaxares II)
653–625	Scythian domination of west Iran
639	Cyrus I succeeds Teispes in Parsumash⁄Anshan; Ariaramnes succeeds Teispes, becomes King of Parsa?
625–585	Cyaxares II (Khuvakhshatra) rules Media; defeats Assyria 612
584–550	Astyages succeeds Cyaxares in Media
550	Cyrus II mentioned in Nabonidus' chronicle as King of Anshan

549   Cyrus II subjugates his cousin Arsames and thereafter is men-
      tioned by Nabonidus as King of Anshan and Parsu (Parsa)

548   Cyrus attacks and defeats Astyages, plunders Ecbatana

547 onwards Cyrus conquers Lydia and establishes Achaemenid empire

CHAPTER I

Metalsmiths and Migrants

IN THE REGION OF LURISTAN in south-west Iran, in the high valleys of the Zagros mountain range, are to be found the remains of an ancient civilisation of which the most striking characteristic is the developed technique of the working of metals, particularly bronze. The range itself, which forms a wall to the east of the Mesopotamian plains, is bisected by the modern Hamadan–Kirmansah road, a route as old as the settlement of man in this area. The configuration of the country on the south of this route, consisting as it does of a series of parallel mountain chains and valleys running from north to south, lay open to the incursions of prehistoric peoples from the the Caspian and Caucasian regions as well as giving oblique access to the Mesopotamian plains. From the burials of the settlers in Luristan has come a rich series of furnishings, mainly of bronze, showing that they expressed their taste in forms strikingly different from those of other ancient Near Eastern peoples. The famous Luristan bronzes, which first became known on the antiquarian market in 1928 and are now abundantly represented in museums and private collections, pose a great many problems not only in archaeology and art-history but also in the history of religious thought.

It is now accepted that the earliest of the bronzes are closely allied to Sumerian types and more particularly to those of Elamite Susa in the plains south-east of the Zagros: picks, axeheads, leaf-shaped daggers similar to types found at Susa, Ur and Tepe Gawra in early dynastic times yet bearing the beginnings of theriomorphic ornament, which was always the peculiarity of Luristan style. Shaft-hole axes with narrowing blades found in Luristan have close analogies in Early Bronze III contexts at Til Barsip in Iraq, Tell Tainat in the plain of

Antioch, and as far away as Poliochni in the isle of Lemnos; thus they belong to a widespread Asiatic type of about 2300 BC. Whilst some allowance must be made for the conservatism of the Luristan metalsmiths, and we cannot rule out the possibility that such early types might have originated in the territory of Susa, and hence had a longer tradition there, the third-millennium origins of the Luristan-Susanian weapons is certified by the existence of a group of inscriptions on vessels and axeheads naming dynastic rulers of the later part of the third millennium. Such objects include a bronze bowl in the Foroughi Collection (Teheran) which is dedicated to Naram Sin, the famous Semitic dynast of Akkad about 2330 BC, a bowl with the dedication to Shargali-Sharri, last king of Akkad (2200 BC), and an axe bearing the name of Addapakshu of Susa in the third dynasty of Ur period (a little before 2000 BC).

There is in fact very little to distinguish those Luristan bronzes which can be ascribed to the earliest period from types current in Elam and Mesopotamia and further afield. Probably they were the products of the first itinerant smiths of the Guti and Lullubi, the earliest people mentioned in cuneiform texts as inhabitants of the Zagros mountains.

The hegemony of the Guti in western Iran and also Iraq from about 2230 to 2090 BC, as indeed the whole course of civilisation in the Near East, was altered by the successive invasions of Caucasian peoples in the early second millennium. Linguistic and archaeological evidence combined acquaints us with three such major movements all of which, whilst basically of Caucasian origin, contained groups of people who either spoke Indo-Aryan dialects or had had prolonged contact with the Indo-Aryan peoples in the steppe-lands north and east of the Caspian. Some were themselves of direct Indo-Aryan origin, forming a ruling aristocracy amongst the new settlers. Of these the Hittites, a branch using the Indo-Aryan Nasili dialect, established themselves in north Anatolia;

then about 1800 a strong folk-movement established a people called the Kassites in the central Zagros and in the flat lands north and east of the confluence of the Diyala and Tigris. By peaceful infiltration the Kassites established their supremacy and in the seventeenth century established a dynasty in Babylon which was to rule with remarkable stability down to the twelfth century B C.

Whilst the Kassites had no literature of which we know and had little artistic influence on Babylonia, we learn from Kassite word lists compiled by Babylonian scribes that their pantheon included, besides personal names of Aryan forms, a number of Indo-Aryan gods.

Yet a third Indo-Aryan migration brought the settlement about the headwaters of the Khabur River of a group of warrior tribes, the Mitanni, who, quick to learn the arts of settled civilisation, established in the sixteenth century a feudal over-lordship over the Hurrian population of north Syria which they later extended to Palestine. Among the Mitanni, Indo-Aryan names were also current; they worshipped deities whose names occur in the Rigveda and used a system of counting which was purely Sanskrit.

All three peoples – the Hittites, Mitanni and Kassites – by virtue of their Caucasian origin had in common a mastery of metalworking, including the knowledge of iron, and a passion for horsemanship. It was the Kassites who introduced to Iran and Mesopotamia a fine breed of horse that superseded the onager, domesticated for traction by the Sumerians, whilst the Mitannian love of horses is attested by numerous surviving texts containing instructions for training horses for the turf. Certainly the high grassy valleys of the Zagros mountains and present-day Kurdistan were perfect breeding grounds for horses and remained so down to Achaemenid times. Certain horsebreeding areas within these regions provided mounts for the Persian army and the Assyrians before them, and the possession of horsebreeding lands played an important role in the struggles between the nascent kingdoms of the Medes and Persians with their Assyrian neighbours.

With the coming of the Kassites, bronze-working in Luristan received fresh impetus. The bronze products of the early part of the second millennium have a distinctly horsey character: rein-rings for guiding the reins along the chariot pole, ornaments for harness, and axeheads shaped like horses' heads with eyes and knots of braided mane down the back of the shaft-hole are the dominant items in the smith's repertory.

Towards the middle of the second millennium, the period when the Kassites were at the peak of their power in Iran and Mesopotamia, there was a distinct falling-off in bronze production. But the revival period, 1100–700 BC, was apparently the most productive for the Luristan bronzes, and it seems that the reconcentration of the Kassites in their mountain homelands after their expulsion from Babylonia, together with a new stream of Caucasian migrants about 1000 BC, gave a new impetus to the metalsmith, who appears to have acquired something of the status of the shaman and magician. By far the largest number of bronzes now come from large single or collective stone-built graves, in which warriors were buried either with their horses or with the horse-bits, harness, weapons and hunting fetishes appertaining to the members of a crude and vicious warrior-hunter society. At the same time, the links now recognisable between Luristan and Caucasian metallurgy are full of significance chronologically and ethnically.

Waves of new invaders who infiltrated into Iran in the closing years of the second millennium were probably impelled by the general stir-up and southward push of the Indo-European peoples of the central and east European steppes, a movement which brought the Dorians to Greece, the Thracians and Phrygians to Asia Minor. People from the eastern Black Sea region were almost certainly pushed southwards over the

Fig. 1. *Luristan short sword of bronze with addorsed ox-heads on the pommel. National Gallery of Victoria. Eighth-seventh centuries BC. Length 14½ in. (28, 31)*

Caucasus. It was certainly from this same region three centuries later that people called *Gimirrai,* or Cimmerians, fell upon Assyria and invaded Asia Minor. These are the Cimmerians whom Herodotus later knew as living on both sides of the Straits of Kertch (the 'Cimmerian Bosphorus' of the Greeks). It is difficult to recognise Cimmerians archaeologically, especially in the earliest phases of the European Iron Age, but perhaps we may legitimately apply, but with no sense of exclusion, the term 'proto-Cimmerian' to these late second-millennium invaders who now had a profound effect on Near Eastern history. Among them were Iranian tribes who introduced to Iran the Aryan language of the Medes and Persians, which is earliest recognised in personal names recorded in eighth-century Assyrian documents. In this early period it was only the areas peripheral to the Mesopotamian world that they were able to occupy; a new power blocked their spread westwards into Syria and Turkey: the Hurrian peoples round Lake Van, who as the millennium progressed were to form the kingdom of Urartu and become a 'world power' on the Near Eastern scene.

Where Luristan weapons are concerned this later period begins with a series of daggers and short swords of types common to Babylonia and Syria. Many of these bear cunei-form dedications, some dozen by Nebuchadnezzar I of Babylon (1146–1123 BC), others by kings of the second dynasty of Isin (1158–1027 BC). Are they the plunder of enemy shrines, re-captured Luristan weapons previously taken and dedicated by Babylonian and Elamite conquerors? This assumption gains some credence from the presence of axeheads with narrow curved blade and spikes on the back of the shaft-hole, a type peculiar to Luristan, bearing inscriptions of similar date.

Fig. 1

21

All these provide good evidence for reinvigoration of bronze-work in the late twelfth century.

As a result of the new migrations from the Caucasus, outside influences on Luristan metalwork now came into prominence. It acquires distinct resemblances to metalwork of the Late Bronze and Early Iron Age in the Koban, central Georgia, Russian Armenia and Azerbaijan, as well as Russian and Persian Talish on the Caspian side. Swords of Talish type, daggers with conical pommels and hanging ornaments of bronze in the form of jingle-bells, open human hands, and miniature animals, solidly cast or of openwork, all derive from Caucasian types, and the hanging ornaments have links even further afield – with the late Bronze Age in Europe and the Dorian invaders of Greece, Thessaly and the Balkans about 1100 BC. That the invaders were horsemen is shown not only by representations of cavalry on seals and bronzes but by the presence in cemetery B at Tepe Siyalk of the curved cheek-pieces of two-link horse bits of Caucasian Iron I type and pierced conical buttons of types later associated with the Thraco-Cimmerians in Hungary and the Ukraine.

Cuneiform texts record that the invasion of Cimmerians proper menaced Urartu in 707 and Assyria in Esarhaddon's reign (681–668 BC). To them may be attributed the introduction to the Luristan repertoire of whetstone handles, shallow metal cups with loop handles riveted on, and U-shaped belt fasteners with spiral terminals. All these have parallels in the final phase (F or Hallstatt B) of the Central European Bronze Age, beginning about 800 BC, and in pre-Etruscan Italy in the same period.

Fig. 2

All the borrowings from and introductions of newcomers were soon transformed, often with subtlety and grace, by the native Luristan animal style. The cheek-pieces of horse bits were cast in the shapes of winged horses, ibexes, bulls and wild boar or occasionally into complicated figurative groups of the animal-lifting demon or animals flanking a sacred tree.

Fig. 2. a–c, Horse bits; d, small amulet, Luristan. Eighth-seventh centuries B C (24)

The ibex, the horse, lionesses, spotted leopards, possibly tigers were the favourite animals. They were chosen not only because of their close relation with the huntsman's life – the ibex is still the 'royal prize' of the Iranian huntsman; lions were still known in Mesopotamia and doubtless leopards in the hills, whilst the horses are slender domesticated beasts wearing bells on collars around their necks – but also because of the Iranian cosmic religion of which these bronzes are the earliest evidence. Sombre bearded gods and puckish horned demons are shown on them, each with animal accompaniments: the ibex, symbol of virility and dominance; the feline, of ferocity and fear; the horse, of wealth and status. Other animals appear: small cervids, wild goats, bears, hares; but domesticated sheep and cattle are rare. These animal-and-demon groups worked into bit-pieces, votive pin-heads and cultic standards are evidence of the animistic and shamanistic beliefs the nomadic hunter derived from his contact with nature: it was a religion where human and feral relationships were closely linked, but the constant repetition of set iconographic themes and a certain consistency of decorative motif certainly suggests the existence of a consecrated priestly caste of which the smiths were the official 'repository artists'.

The most intricate of the cast metalwork objects are the so-called 'cultic standards'. Each consists of a central anthropo-

Fig. 3. Bronze cultic standard from Luristan. Cincinnati Art Museum. Eighth-seventh centuries B C. Height 7¼ in. (11, 34)

morphic figure, rather tubular in appearance and about nine inches high, flanked by a pair of flatly modelled rearing feline creatures, which arch their heads over towards the head of the anthropoid figure between them. This figure usually stretches out its hands to grasp the neck of the felines and often sub/sidiary animals (dogs or birds of prey) are attached to the backs of these, thus forming an integrated and not ungraceful group. Over fifty of these standards are known and in the majority of pieces the characteristics of the anthropomorphic central figure are female, or at least androgynous: occasionally she places hands to breasts in the fertility posture; she dominates and nurtures the animal kingdom, both the lions (king of beasts) and the hawks as well as the dogs which prey upon the lions and keep, so to speak, the balance of nature. She is a cosmic figure and, without pushing too far into the unknown, we must see her as embodying the chief life/giving principle for gods and men and animals. Her fertility is symbolized by either moufflon horns or phallic/tip attached to her head, her genitivity by the three or more human heads attached to the column below her own, heads which represent either lower members of the divine hierarchy or human or divine life issuing from her womb.

An entirely different aspect of later Luristan culture, and one important for the emerging picture of the prehistoric back/ground of Median and Achaemenid civilisation, was revealed by the excavations at the temple site at Surkh Dum. Here in 1938 E. Schmidt excavated a primitive building with numer/ous *ex/voto* offerings consisting chiefly of pins with circular disc/shaped heads with embossed decoration, belonging to an iconographic tradition differing considerably from that of the cast metalwork. These pins as well as some shield bosses and belt/plaques are now known in considerable quantities from Surkh Dum, Kuh/i Dasht and the surrounding Pish/i Kuh valley region south of Kirmansah. They show, contrary to

Fig. 3

Fig. 4

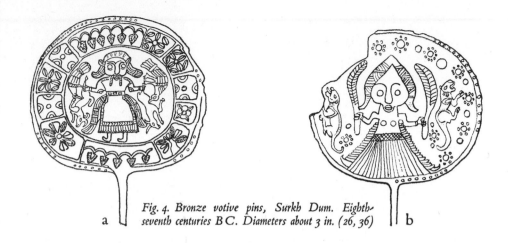

a

b

Fig. 4. Bronze votive pins, Surkh Dum. Eighth-
seventh centuries BC. Diameters about 3 in. (26, 36)

frequent supposition, that the decorators of the pins knew in
part the same hunting existence and the same demons as the
bronze-casters: some correspondence in motif and dress can
certainly be shown. Nevertheless, the art of the pin-heads and
other pieces of engraved and embossed metal was predominantly
the art of a priestly caste concerned with the portrayal of cosmic
beliefs and religious ceremonies in a style remotely dependent
on the art of Assyria and involving techniques now known not
to have been limited to Luristan but also practised in Persian
Kurdistan, Azerbaijan, and in the Elburz valleys south of the
Caspian and incorporating elements of design from the metalworking centres of Urartu on Lake Van. The present indications are that the decorative and iconographic elements
peculiar to the pins and plaques of Surkh Dum style are far
more widespread in the mountain valleys of western Iran than
the Luristan cast metalwork, but its implications will be more
fully discussed in the next chapter.

For the purpose of placing this earliest repoussé metal
decoration in a significant context in pre-Achaemenid civilisation, it is sufficient to outline the possible interpretation of
groups of Indo-Aryan religious themes depicted upon them.

Fig. 5. Repoussé quiver sheath, Kuh-i Dasht. Metropolitan Museum, New York. Height 21 in. (18, 21)

Fig. 5

Firstly René Dussaud saw the depiction on pin-heads and belt-strips of the *haoma* festival and cults of specifically Mithraic type and recognised that certain figures were holding the barsom, a bundle of sacred twigs carried by worshippers in pre-Zoroastrian religious practice. Evidence supplied by their sparse surviving literature, supplemented by a considerable body of theophoric personal names, shows that the Kassites had worshipped the sun and war gods of the Rigveda, Suriash and Marutash, Buriash, a storm god, and probably the Vedic Indra, also mentioned in Mitanni texts. They shared the three-fold hierarchy of divinities (divided into gods of sky, atmos-phere and earth) of early Vedic religion, which Zoroastrianism later spiritualized. A Luristan bronze plaque from a Kuh-i Dasht quiver with its three superimposed panels of divine figures certainly appears to illustrate such a concept. The twin gods in the top panel (sky) are probably Mitra (Mithras) and Varuna, the closely associated sovereign gods of world order; Mitra with his cosmic bull, Varuna with his small square fire-altar. Below these in the central panel (atmosphere) is Indra, chief of the Vedic Mārutas, the gods of power, storm, and war. Indra, as in the Rigveda, is here accompanied by lions and a bird of prey (*senya*) and to demonstrate his secondary role as a hunting god he holds two slain goats, spoils of the chase, for he is made equivalent to the war-and-hunting god Ninurta in Akkadian texts. In the lowest register (earth) appear the twin Nāsatyas, healers, rejuvenators and gods of fecundity. Here they appear in the act of playing, and rejuven-ating the old man Chyavāna (Rigveda 1, 116, 10) who holds his new and well-coiffured head ready for placement.

Fig. 6. Repoussé scabbard sheath, Luristan. Private Collection. Height 24 in. (115)

The repetition of this three-fold division of the field on similarly decorated pieces shows that, even if this cosmic interpretation is erroneous, at least the explanation of the themes lies along lines wholly foreign to Mesopotamian religion. The same can be said of a frequently represented theme which is more controversial: a horned and bearded god with ample robe and drooping wings bears twin human or dragon figures upon his shoulders, at the same time holding sprouts of greenery in his outstretched hands. The fullest representation is on a silver strip in the Cincinnati Museum, but other representations on pin-heads and shield bosses are known.

Fig. 6

Plates 4, 5

Miss P. Ackerman explained the central figure of the Cincin-nati plaque as the great father god equivalent to the Canaanite El, a bull and mountain god, giving birth to the Asvins, the Indian equivalent of the classical Dioscuri or Castor and Pollux, shown like their classical counterparts being born from eggs and surrounded by votaries in the 'three ages of man' – squatting children, standing youths and bearded elders all clasping the long-stemmed palm which appears to be the distinctive attribute of divinity in Luristan art. For Professor Ghirshman the central figure is that of Zurvan, the Iranian father god of time here seen in the act of giving birth to the twin Asuras, the opposing principles of good and evil.

Plate 4

Both interpretations leave much detail unexplained and force cultural and chronological connexions, but again we may be certain that Iranian duality lies behind these remarkably consistent representations.

Whatever the interpretations, there is certainly an icono-graphic unity in the plaques depicting religious themes. Deities, usually winged, and priests, usually with the barsom tied around their waists, wear the same calf-length robe ending in a deep fringe. Over it is worn a crossed stole or pair of braces ending at the waist. In addition to the isolated cultic

Fig. 7. *Part of a gold belt plaque from Luristan. Private Collection. Eighth century BC. Total length 17¼ in., width 2⅜ in. (21)*

Fig. 7

Plates 1, 2

a

b

scenes, always difficult to interpret, a number of belt-plaques in bronze and gold show processions of priests leading animals and preparing braziers for those bloody sacrifices which Zoroaster was later to forbid, and even mixing *haoma*, the sacred intoxicating drink, which again Zoroaster condemned. It is perhaps in these plaque and pin representations that we catch our only surviving glimpse of the Magi who controlled aspects of Iranian religion through Median and Achaemenid times.

Assyrian influence on beaten metalwork began to predominate in the late eighth century BC, probably as the result of the presence in the central Zagros of Assyrian garrisons (especially at Kharkhar and Bit Kari) during the reigns of Sargon II (722–705) and Esarhaddon. Progressive Assyrian influence is especially shown in a series of drinking beakers or situlae, which appear to have been produced originally at a centre in the old Kassite territory around Bit Humban or Kar Kashi in the ninth century BC. Their style is remarkably unified and many of them portray enthroned bearded princes partaking of banquets and served by their courtiers and musicians. They wear a decorative version of Babylonian court dress and use Babylonian furniture, both adopted by the Kassites during their rule in Babylon. But the weapons, musical instruments and decoration of the robes are all Iranian and the details depict for us the courts of the petty nomadic princelings. More rarely, shields and other items have come to light decorated in

c   Fig. 8. *Animal figures from Luristan situlae*

Fig. 9. Banquet scene engraved on a Luristan situla. Ninth-eighth centuries B C. Private Collection. (52)

the same 'banquet style'. A ceremonial cauldron in the Cincinnati Museum provides a link between native Luristan cast metalwork and the embossed situlae. The later situlae boldly copy Assyrian motifs including antithetic bearded bulls Plate 3 and sacred emblems, though often with slight deviations from Assyrian style. Undoubtedly these later situlae were made before Esarhaddon's hold on these eastern territories Fig. 8 crumbled in 672 B C. We must certainly bear these vessels in mind when we come to consider the predominant Assyrian inspiration of Medo-Achaemenid art, for the evidence suggests that they were made at a time and place close to the formation of the Median kingdom. Indeed, it is quite possible that the figures we see embossed on them are those of early Median princelings.

Despite the difficulty of understanding and explaining Luristan art, its role in founding an Iranian tradition is of paramount importance. Median and Achaemenid art cannot be explained without reference to it. It was, like these, an animal art aiming at symmetry and balance with a tendency to reduce all forms to a two-part pattern. Where the external forms made such a balance difficult, this was compensated for by exaggerating internal details, by the artificial delineation of limbs and muscles, by overemphasizing folded skin and patterned hair, or breaking up the body into component parts, until often all sense of organic structure was lost. It was symptomatic of the duality which lay at the heart of Iranian character and which pervaded all forms of Achaemenid expression.

CHAPTER II

Mannai, Medes and Scythians

AS IS ONLY TO BE EXPECTED, the entry of these waves of barbarian nomads into the spheres of the settled and highly evolved urban civilisations of upper Mesopotamia, north Syria and south-eastern Anatolia changed their cultural and artistic alignment. Only in recent years have archaeological excavations in the regions of the south-west Caspian and south of Lake Urmiya made it possible to study the amalgam of nomadic and sedentary arts which these incursions produced in Iran. A series of archaeological discoveries, whilst setting profound problems, adds a new dimension to our thinking about the Luristan culture and the genesis of Achaemenid art. The very recent discoveries at Amlash, Daylaman, Marlik Tepe and Hasanlu yielded documents of early Iranian art whose precise identity has yet to be determined; their most unifying feature is dependence upon the animal form for basic decorative elements. This art is an expression of the animal art of the Eurasian steppes modified by Mesopotamian, Hittite and Urartian contacts; for the Vannic kingdom of Urartu was the nearest western neighbour of the lands settled by the nomads in the Caspian and Azerbaijan regions. In the eighth century Urartu was to unify politically, and to some extent culturally, the entire west of Anatolia and north Syria, taking in the strong and independent Syro-Hittite kingdoms of south-east Turkey and the Aramaean kingdoms around Aleppo. In the beginning of the first millennium, however, specific influence from any of these latter sources is absent and, at least from the Caspian side of the area under discussion, the discoveries link with the Caucasus on the one hand and with certain aspects of Luristan metalwork on the other. Tentatively we might regard a group of them that come from sites in the provinces of

Mazanderan and Gilan bordering the south-west shore of the Caspian as belonging to a folk basically 'proto-Cimmerian'.

Of these, the only one known to us from anything but clandestine or unscientific digging is Marlik Tepe (Gilan), in the valley of the Gohar-Rudh, north-west of Rasht. Dug into the hillside were a number of funerary chambers in which the sparse and scattered bones of the dead were found accompanied by remains of rich metalwork and pottery. This, together with the enormous size of some of the shallow-built chambers (e.g. $16\frac{1}{2} \times 10$ ft) constructed in the excrescences of natural rock, suggests that here were tombs of chieftains or of a royal dynasty. Outstanding among the grave goods were a number of gold and silver vessels, pieces of jewellery and weapons.

Fig. 10

By far the major part of the material belonging to what might now be called the 'Mazanderan Culture' comes from the area around two villages in Gilan province called Amlash and Daylaman, situated in the high (2,000 m.) valleys east of the Sefid Rud. All the known pieces derive from investigations of tombs by local peasants. Amongst those acquired by museums and reputable dealers is a high proportion which corresponds closely to the Marlik Tepe finds and appears to represent a single cultural period of about 900 BC, when the northern and western slopes of the Elburz were occupied by a people of advanced taste and of an artistic individuality remarkably unaffected by Mesopotamian influences.

Fig. 11

Plates 8, 14

The freedom of their creative approach is best shown in a series of pottery jugs of a fine crimson slipped and polished fabric shaped like humped bulls (the domesticated zebu) or red deer, the bodies completely enclosed except for a channel spout the opening of which lies along the top of the head. These are masterpieces of the potter's craft, the animals sculpturesque and dynamic in shape, sinuous and uncluttered, worthy of a Brancusi, Hepworth or Moore. The curvature of the humps, rumps and hollow backs of the bulls is pleasingly

Fig. 10. a–c, Gold vessels from Marlik Tepe. Ninth–eighth centuries B C; d, griffin from a Marlik bowl (54–56)

Fig. 11. Beakers of precious metal; a, b, from Amlash; c, from Marlik Tepe; d, beaker with gold-encrusted battle scene from Hasanlu. Ninth century B C. Height 6¾ in. (44, 115)

offset by a sharp edge along the outer edge of the hump or along the dewlap; the graceful line of the turned neck of the deer, by the intricate stumpy horns. They share one quality with animals in Balkan and Russian folk-art, a certain '*Bäuerlich-keit*'. A series of jugs, some in the shape of horses of which one comes from Makou on the Iranian-Turkish border, might be related to the bull jugs.

Plates 9-12

It is also chiefly stags and humped cattle that are represented by small model animals of cast bronze. Considerable quantities of these come from Amlash and examples from Marlik and Khurvin – bronze hanging ornaments, small animals and pomegranate-shaped jingle-bells – would seem to belong to an early Cimmerian metalwork tradition already noted at Siyalk and Luristan. A bronze horseman is of some significance, since the proto-Cimmerians undoubtedly introduced the use of the horse as a mount, and a cylinder seal of particularly barbaric style showing a mounted warrior was found in one of the Siyalk B cemetery graves.

Plates 13, 15

These pottery and bronze animals in particular link the Mazanderan materials with those found early this century in the megalithic graves of the northern adjoining regions of Talish and Lenkoran, which span the close of the Bronze Age late in the second millennium BC and the opening of the Iron Age. Pottery animal vases, although inferior to those of Mazanderan, and bronze suspension animals, mostly deer, are common in such graves as those at Agha-Evlar in Persian Talish, Razgur in Russian Lenkoran, Tulu in Russian Talish and Samthavro in the Caucasus, whilst here and in other Caucasian graveyards the same bells and openwork bronze ornaments are found. The swords of Kalar Dasht and Marlik Tepe are of Talish type (with a crescent spanning the midrib on the top of the blade) and even the earrings decorated with clusters of miniature gold grapes and pomegranates and the circular gold medallions with cruciform and stellate designs found at

Marlik and Amlash have parallels at Redkin Lager and Lschasen north of Lake Sevan and Veri in Russian Talish. There can be little doubt that the Mazanderan culture is basically an extension of the southward migration of the late Bronze Age cultures of the Caucasus and Transcaucasian steppes in eastern Soviet Azerbaijan.

It has already been claimed that there are certain links between Mazanderan culture and Luristan. This is particularly evident in the series of golden beakers and bowls from Amlash and Marlik Tepe. These have many of the decorative devices of Luristan beaten metal cups, the rosette under the base, and single or double torsade decoration engraved on the lip, an attractive and peculiarly Iranian device found in all types of Luristan beaten metal. The elongated conical golden goblets with horizontal ribs from Amlash and Marlik are shaped precisely like vessels found at Zulu Ab in Luristan, and the bulls processing round a magnificent golden beaker from Marlik Tepe have arched necks and feathered joints exactly like animals on Luristan horse bits. Behind the bulls is the same filling ornament of stars and florets common in Luristan. On the whole, however, the decoration of the beakers from the northern sites is richer and more carefully drawn than any⁄thing in Luristan and it seems probable that the beakers and the artistic traditions they display were being carried southwards rather than vice⁄versa. The striding animals they depict have the arched necks and compartmented bodies of those seen on belt⁄plaques in Georgian and Koban tombs of the twelfth century.

Important Mesopotamian strains in metal decoration from northern sites impinge upon the simple animal style. A theme of cosmic importance, a double⁄headed lion⁄eagle grasping a young gazelle in merciless talons, is strikingly portrayed on an electrum beaker acquired by the Louvre. Whilst the basic conception of such a monster is probably Mesopotamian, its

Fig. 10

Fig. 11c,
Fig. 2

Plates 7, 8

Fig. 6

Fig. 10. a, d

form is unique in the art of western Asia. It is strikingly matched by the monster on a Luristan quiver. Another group of Amlash-Marlik vessels, probably considerably later in date (perhaps 800–750 BC), have high-beaten reliefs in a peculiarly rococo and slightly comic version of Assyrian art, yet certainly with individual artistic qualities.

In these finds we appear to have products resulting from that same series of Iranian invasions of the early part of the first millennium to which we have attributed certain developments in Luristan. These settlers with their developed metal tech-niques and grey or black polished pottery imitating metal shapes, particularly flasks and spouted pitchers, can now be traced not only at Tepe Giyan, Tepe Siyalk and Luristan in the south of Iran but in the new Caspian sites, at Khurvin in Qazvin province, Geoy Tepe in Azerbaijan, and Hasanlu, south-west of Lake Urmiya near Solduz.

The native arts of these people, like those of Luristan, came more and more under Assyrian influence until they were finally eclipsed. Of the movements and distributions of these tribes little can be said, but it seems certain that out of this rich and fluid cultural background the art and civilisation of the Medes crystallised in the eighth century BC.

Whilst poor in stratigraphic and historical information, the period is yet rich in treasure. One of the most interesting monu-ments of religious iconography discovered in the Ancient Near East in recent years is the golden bowl from Hasanlu (Persian Kurdistan). This ancient citadel-mound, excavated in 1956–8 by R. Dyson of the University of Pennsylvania appears to have been occupied since the early third millennium BC. But the most interesting finds derive from a later period, 1000–750 BC, when Hasanlu was an important centre within the territory of a people called the Mannai in Assyrian inscrip-tions. The land of Manna lay in the hill region east of Sulai-maniyah.

In the south-west of the Hasanlu citadel, buildings of the city's penultimate phase, characterised chiefly by the grey, polished channel-spouted pottery of northern type, had been destroyed suddenly by fire. Among the debris of the collapsed two-storey buildings were found metalwork and glazed tiles of types in use in Assyrian palaces in the ninth century BC. In one room the debris had collapsed upon three soldiers making their escape with looted objects. The leader of the group held an iron sword with a gold-inlaid hilt, a second a bronze-fluted sceptre, the third was carrying the golden bowl which slipped from his hands as he fell to the ground under the burning beams.

The perpetrators of this destruction, so dramatically un-covered by the spade, were undoubtedly the Urartians, whose own civilisation has been the subject of much research and discovery in recent years. Two stone inscriptions of Urartian origin have been found in the Hasanlu region. The first, a stela from Kel-i shin, was set up by King Ishpuini of Urartu and his son Menuas (815–807 BC); the second, from Tashtepe, 80 km. east of Hasanlu, celebrates the conquest of the Manna state by Menuas II of Urartu (804–790 BC). A date between 815 and 790 is therefore likely for the death of the plunderers; this accords well with the Carbon 14 analysis of material from the robbers' 'grave'.

The bowl is undoubtedly of Iranian manufacture, with torsaded rim and intricate 'storied' sides displaying the Iranian techniques of animal delineation and filling ornament. The physiognomy and dress of human beings on the bowl are close to both Amlash and Luristan types. Further proof of the local manufacture of the bowl is provided by the Talish swords to be seen beneath one of the chariots on the upper frieze of its decoration.

Plate 6

This upper frieze depicts the three Hurrian gods in chariots drawn by bulls and mules and is reminiscent of weather gods on Hurri-Mitanni cylinder seals of the later second millennium from Syria and south-east Turkey. Miss Porada and others have conjectured that the apparently disconnected themes which occupy the spaces below the encircling frieze of the weather gods are illustrations of some Hurrian mythological story, possibly the Ullikummis myth. The close relationship with the technique of the Amlash and Marlik beakers must be stressed.

Fig. 11d

A tall silver beaker with electrum-overlaid figures from the same burnt building at Hasanlu has a lower frieze of Marlik-type animals and a battle scene around the rim with infantry and charioteers, a reflection of the troubles portending Hasanlu's end. The physiognomy of these warriors recalls that of the figures on the bowl. The heads are narrow and bound with fillets: the hair falls long and untrimmed down the back of the head.

There is yet another and larger treasure from Manna terri-tory: this is the now famous treasure of Ziwiyeh, a mound of ruins south-east of Lake Urmiya. In 1947 the inhabitants of the near-by village of Sakkiz found a hoard of gold, silver and ivory in a bath-shaped coffin. The original hoard was cut up by peasants; consequently it is far from certain how much was in the coffin hoard and how much is due to later operations at the mound. The nucleus of the hoard was homogeneous neither in techniques nor styles and it is now possible to see distinct divisions.

Fig. 16
Plates 16, 17, 19–25

Plates 21, 22

Recognition for artistic consistency should first be given to the gold plaques, sheaths and ivory pieces engraved in purely Assyrian style and largely concerned with lion-hunt scenes, Assyrian in every detail, stolid, dull and repetitious. Secondly,

Plate 20

there belong together a crescentic gold pectoral and parts of three trapezoidal breast-plates all engraved with rows of fantastic animals flanking sacred trees. Here again the con-ception is basically Assyrian, but the art is rather an amalgam of several traits in which some borrowings from Phoenicia,

Fig. 12

Fig. 12. Part of a trapezoidal gold plaque from Ziwiyeh, probably a breast-plate. Metropolitan Museum, New York. The complete plaque with six rows of animals measured 10¼ in. wide (top) to 5⅝ in. (bottom); height 11½ in. (51, 121)

more from Urartu, are discernible. The crescentic pectoral is itself Urartian in shape and so are the horned and winged lions and hideous eagle-griffins included in the bestiary. The custom of making demons composed of parts of various animals was particularly pronounced in Urartu.

The crescentic pectoral serves as the best introduction to a third stylistic division, for in the narrow ends of the crescent crouch animals in purely Scythian style: hares and bears, their limbs ending or 'melting' into the curly feet of animals from the later Scythian workshops on the Russian steppe. Other gold fragments from the treasure have marginal rows of griffin heads, a popular device with Scythian artists, and there is also an intriguing piece of gold foil (now fragmented in about 24 pieces) covered with a lattice-work of tresses, which are in reality the curly-ended branches of a sacred tree. In the inter- *Fig. 13* stices of the branches are miniature crouched stags of Scythian form, exactly as in pieces from the great Scythian finds at Kul Oba and the Dniepr region. The junctures of the sacred branches are covered by Urartian lion masks. This plaque compares with other pieces of a mixed Urartian style, from

Zakim in the Turkish province of Kars and Ani Pemza in Soviet Armenia, in one of which the tresses enfold Urartian animals whilst the other is bordered by a typically Urartian-styled tree. A recent find of a Urartian belt in an Iron Age grave at Tli in Osetia is yet another illustration of the popularity of Urartian objects amongst peripheral peoples.

Obviously we are dealing with a period of common interchange between Iran, Urartu and south Russian Scythian principalities. Amongst the objects from Ziwiyeh which do not belong to the treasure are actual Scythian imports: a stone weight or seal purely Scythian in form of a type found at the Urartian town of Karmir Blur in Erivan, which the Scythians overran in 625 BC, and in the Scythian homeland of Kelermes and other burial sites; and the curved cheek-piece of a horse bit terminating in an animal head, a type with three bridle-holes which is peculiar to the Scyths. Like these, however, the most

Plate 25

significant Scythian piece, a silver bowl encrusted with concentric circles of Scythian animals and griffin heads arranged round a central circle of Assyrian lotus-buds, cannot with certainty be attributed to the main hoard.

These Scythian objects constitute one of the most difficult and controversial problems posed by the treasure, but the presence of direct Scythian imports as well as the presence of Scythian animals on more local work appears to place the Ziwiyeh finds in the period 675–625 BC when the Scythians ruled Mannaean territory. But this date is seemingly early for the objects which have exact parallels in Scythian tombs in the Russian homeland. The Assyrian and Urartian influences in certain objects may be assumed to pre-date 612, when the Medes decisively defeated the Assyrians, and certainly 590, when Karmir Blur was destroyed. The objections based on Scythian chronology might be met by the suggestion that Scythian art, which hitherto has been regarded as an indigenous development of the steppe-lands, did in fact develop

Fig. 13. Part of a gold plaque with Scythian animals from Ziwiyeh. The complete original was 6½ in. wide (39, 49, 51)

south of the Caucasus under Mesopotamian impact during the period of Scythian domination, spreading into south Russia in the early sixth century, thus beginning the close link between Scythian and Iranian art. The lines for such a development are plausibly suggested by the style-analysis of some of the objects, but much depends on the date of the burial of the treasure. Even though the coffin itself and some of its contents were made early in the seventh century (i.e. before Scythian domination), the ivories do not appear to be earlier than Esarhaddon's reign and the parallels to the Assyrianising Ziwiyeh plaques from Khafantlu, 3 miles to the south-west of Ziwiyeh, show that we are not dealing with isolated heir-looms. The *burial* of the treasure might, however, have taken place in the subsequent reign of Assurbanipal (668–626), late enough to have included objects of the newly-developed Scythian style. The attribution of the treasure to Esarhaddon's reign is further suggested by the known dealings of this monarch with the Scythians. Early in his reign he himself married his daughter to a Scythian prince. Whilst we know nothing of Ziwiyeh's history in his reign, Sargon II before him,

Plate 18

41

and Assurbanipal after him, campaigned against the Mannai and took Izibie and Izirtu, probably Ziwiyeh and Khafantlu. Possibly the two first-named towns housed Scythian garrisons, for an alliance between Scythians and Mannai under Scythian leadership had taken place about 675 B C.

The cities of Urartu, too, felt the brunt of the Scythian invasion in the later years of the seventh century and the archaeological evidence of Karmir Blur confirms this. Before the Scythians overran Van there must have been a period of peaceful intercourse between the Urartians, Mannai and their future conquerors.

Joining the fragmentary patchwork of art and culture made up by these valuable discoveries are certain threads of historical data gleaned from Assyrian annals. It appears, for instance, that the Mannai, whatever their racial identity, were in the first three-quarters of the eighth century a power potent enough to draw off the warlike preoccupations of Assyria and Urartu alike. In the century between the successful campaigns of Sargon II against them and the fall of the Scythian garrisons in Mannai territory, we hear nothing of them as a racial entity and it is probable that the Ziwiyeh objects, with one exception, in no way reflect the native Mannaean background. This

Plate 23

exception is an ivory plaque engraved *en creux* with the scene of a king either receiving booty or preparing for war. He stands under a parasol receiving a staff-bearer and armourer with bow and arrows, whilst another figure leads off a bull. Copied from an Assyrian source (parasol and sacred tree) it is charm-ingly rendered in Iranian style: the long-fringed garments with embroidered side-panels are found on Luristan beaten metal-

Fig. 7

work and especially on a series of gold and bronze belt-plaques showing processions of figures in ritual ceremonies, all in the same crude style as on the Ziwiyeh ivory. They use a set of artistic conventions which linked Luristan and the Mannai territory, and in this light it seems possible that the inhabitants of these two regions in the first millennium were derived from the same Iranian folk movement. Closely implicated with the political history of both Mannai and Luristanians in the seventh century were the two Iranian tribes who were soon to dominate all western Iran.

Unknown in second-millennium history, the tribal names 'Madai' and 'Parsua', the inseparable Medes and Persians of the Greeks, occur first in the Assyrian historical records of the ninth century BC. Rulers of these two tribes paid tribute to Assyria in the reign of Shalmaneser III (869–824) and at that time the Parsua appear to have been located south and south-west of Lake Urmiya, the Madai south-eastwards of the eastern slopes of the northern Kurdistan hills, spreading eastwards on to the north-western plateau, somewhat to the north of the area which was known as Media in Achaemenid times. The Parsua meanwhile moved down the Zagros spine and established a second enclave in the central Zagros in territories where Assyria claimed control. Sargon II established Assyrian garrisons within 'Parsuash' territory, chief of which was Kharkhar ('Fort Sargon') not far from modern Hamadan. In Sargon's time, however, the Parsua were already occupying the valleys in the Bakhtiari foothills west of Shustar and north-east of Susa, not far from the Elamite territory of Anshan. This new settlement area they called Parsumash and gradually the bulk of the Parsua settled there and eventually took over the Anshan territory from the tottering Elamite kingdom. But in 692 we still hear of Parsumash and Anshan battling as associated allies against Assyria's King Sennacherib.

Given every opportunity by the weakness of Shalmaneser V (727–722), the Medes became an increasingly important factor in Assyrian politics. It is, however, very unlikely that before the reign of Sargon their primitive tribal organisation permitted any concerted political action. We hear that a local Median chieftain, Daiaukku, who opposed Sargon in 715 BC, was

Fig. 14

considered powerful enough to merit deportation to one of the Assyrian-controlled cities in Syria. He is probably the Deioces who is said by Herodotus to have been the original unifier of the Median kingdom and the founder of Ecbatana. What precisely Daiaukku's achievement was, his relationship with the Parsua, whether in fact he was strictly a Mede at all – none of this we know. But after Sargon's reign, in 702 BC, a Median king, Ukshatar (Greek: Cyaxares), attacked the Assyrian garrison at Kharkhar.

The difficulties with the refractory Mannai may have led the Assyrians in Esarhaddon's reign to collect supplies and horses from the Madai. Previously Zamua had been the main source of supply, but though ever loyal to Assyria, the province was under threat from the Mannai on its eastern borders. Ever since the days of Shalmaneser's raids, operations in Madai territory had been hazardous, although Tiglathpileser III (746–728) had gathered tribute from it. But it now appears that Assyrian intervention in Median affairs was not entirely unwelcome, for when Esarhaddon's forces began to penetrate their territory, three chieftains presented themselves at Nineveh between campaigns to secure his help against rebellions at home. They were Uppis of Partakka, Zanasanna of Partukka and Ramataia of Urukazabarna. The first of these place-names – Partakka – is probably the origin of the later central Iranian province of Parthia, but its whereabouts at this period is unknown. All these territories lay well beyond Assyrian-controlled Zamua and Parsuash, and the request for Assyrian protection in land apparently settled by the Medes and the return of a handsome tribute suggests that the unification of the Medes under Deioces, as told by Herodotus, was a fiction of later times. In 676 BC an Assyrian raid penetrated Median territory as far as Mount Bikni (Demavend, north-east of Teheran) in the district of Patusharri, and between 676 and 673 raids into this area were intensified. It is of course possible that the route of the Assyrian

Fig. 14. *Assyria and Persia in eighth-seventh centuries B C*

armies lay to the south of Madai territory, but interference from Medes and Cimmerians was certainly expected.

By 672 BC Esarhaddon appears to have achieved a degree of genuine stability on his eastern borders, but oracular texts show his growing concern from 674 onwards with the activities of a certain Kashtaritu, who had begun to unite the Mannaean, Median and newly arrived Cimmerian forces and further threatened the already weak security of tribute from Manna. Kashtaritu appears to have been king of Kar Kashi in the central Zagros, whose basic population was still the Kassite remnant. He has, for good reason, been identified by modern scholars as none other than the Phraortes of Herodotus and son of Cyaxares, who is said to have been the first to make the Persians subject to the Medes. Kashtaritu took Dur Enlil and Sharru Iqbi, the two chief Mannaean towns, from Assyrian control and held sway over Manna until the campaign of Assurbanipal after 660 BC restored Assyrian dominance there. Of Phraortes' subjection of Teispes of the Parsua we have no contemporary evidence, but the circumstances of Cyrus' relations with Assurbanipal which will be mentioned in the next chapter suggests its likelihood.

These initial skirmishes between Assyrians and Medes took place in territory ranging from the Caspian to the Persian Gulf. Urartu and Elam were both implicated and Manna was used as a puppet by Urartians and Medes alike, whilst the Scythians took any advantage they could of the current situation, mostly as Cimmerian subsidiaries.

These circumstances account for the mixture of styles in the Ziwiyeh pieces, and we must bear them in mind when seeking the beginning of a specifically Median art. What, then, is the significance of the main objects of the Ziwiyeh treasure, the crescentic pectoral and the trapezoidal plates, attributable exclusively to neither an Assyrian nor a Urartian or Scythian or Mannaean source? Without wishing to cut the coat too

Fig. 15. Glazed faience box found at Susa. c. 700 B C. Height about 8 in.

closely to fit the cloth, can we attribute them to the art of the Medes, who have hitherto remained in the shadows of first-millennium history, or to the Parsua to whose central Zagros territory we may tentatively attribute the Luristan situlae and the Susa and Tchoga Zambil faience plaques and boxes which share the same animal style? Undoubtedly we should not at this stage dogmatise about a specifically Median form of art, yet the situlae, faiences and Ziwiyeh gold plaques certainly share the same eclectic attitude to Assyrian sources, have some of the same mythical animals, the same fashion of rows of animals *passant*; and certainly in the Ziwiyeh plates and Luristan situlae and plaques the drawing of animal's rib-cages as upcurving triangles fastened to the top of the pelvis by a 'button' is a mannerism which we shall see continued on the threshold of Achaemenid art. It seems likely that Median art originated in this 'mixed style' which we find in the northern and central Zagros.

Of the physical appearance and dress of the Medes during this early period, Assyrian art has left us a general but not absolutely consistent picture. Sargonid reliefs depict them as

Fig. 8

Fig. 15

Fig. 16. Median tribute-bearers engraved on the rim of the bronze coffin from Ziwiyeh (58)

Fig. 16

medium-sized and short-haired, wearing sheepskin cloaks or leopard-skin capes. They wear laced boots reaching the calf, pointed caps with broad forehead-bands or falling into three folds – in short, the expected clothing of men from chilly regions. Men of very similar appearance with fringed (wool-lined?) and spotted (leopard-skin?) mantles are etched on the rim of the bronze sarcophagus in which the Ziwiyeh treasure was found.

CHAPTER III

Builders of Empire

IT WAS NOT LONG before these peripheral encounters brought the Medes to close grips with the Assyrian forces. The ascendency of Phraortes (Khshathrita, the Kashtaritu of Assyrian texts) was short-lived: a new tribe, stemming from the Parsua, soon prevailed over the southern branch of the Persians in Parsumash. Its leader was Hakamanish, the eponymous father of the line of Hakamanish, or Achaemenes, as the Greeks called him; and from the time of his grandson Ariaramna (Ariaramnes) survives the first historical inscription in Persian (written in cuneiform) relating to the Achaemenids. It gives the descent of Ariaramna and his brother Kurash (Cyrus I) and their father Chishpish (Teispes) from Haka-manish. Teispes himself in this inscription bears the titles 'Great King, King of Anshan' (Anzan), the Elamite name for the area north and east of Susa in modern Khuzistan. Possibly his name is the same as that of a certain Cimmerian leader Teushpa named in the record of Esarhaddon's year 678. The terms of Ariaramnes' inscription leave no doubt that whilst

Fig. 17

Fig. 17. Gold-plaque inscription of Ariaramnes in Old Persian cuneiform script, found at Hamadan (6, 70)

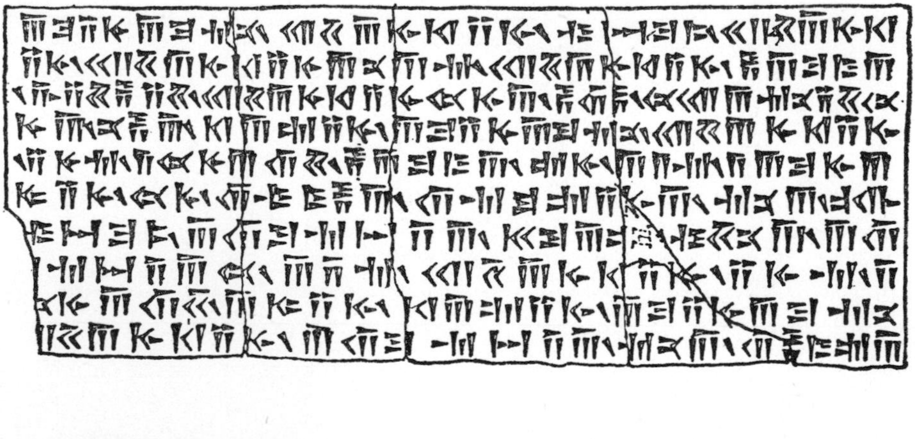

this area was the central homeland of the Achaemenid house it was far from being completely subdued before Teispes' time. Possibly the Parsua were still moving southwards and had taken this area from the Elamites. Furthermore, Ariaramnes significantly records how the god Ahuramazda gave him *Parsa* 'great of horses, great of men', thereby providing the first Persian record of the name of the Aryan supreme god. The inscription also indicates that Ariaramnes had taken posses-sion of the land south-east of Parsumash and Anshan, of Parsa (modern Fars, around Shiraz). To his brother Cyrus he gives only his father's title 'King of Anshan', taking for himself the more ambitious one 'King of Kings, King of Parsa'. It is not known under what circumstances the territories of the Parsua were divided between his two sons on Teispes' death. The division implied in this inscription from Ecbatana – if it be genuinely a contemporary record and not a fake of later times – accords with later titles in the Nabonidus chronicle.

Ariaramnes' territorial ambitions outside the Parsumash–Anshan area and Parsa in the south had received a consider-able setback from the coalition of the northern Medes with the Scythians and Cimmerians under Phraortes-Kashtaritu who, as previously said, subdued the Achaemenid Teispes to vassalage. The united Median-Cimmerian-Scythian forces swept the south and, amongst other things, carried off Ariara-mna's gold-tablet inscription to the important Median centre of Ecbatana (or Agamtana in Assyrian cuneiform, and modern Hamadan). Phraortes formed an anti-Assyrian coalition and met defeat and death at the hands of Assurbanipal's army in 653 BC.

Whilst Parsa had fallen to the Medes, Cyrus was still in command in Parsumash and Anshan and, having established his independence of the Medes upon Phraortes' death, he paid tribute to Assurbanipal at Nineveh, although his real sym-pathies lay with the rebel king Shamash-shum-ukin of

Babylon rather than with the Assyrians. Cyrus could expect little Assyrian support against the Median threat to the Parsua kingdom, and after Assurbanipal's death in 626 a new and better equipped Median army organised by Cyaxares II, son and successor of Phraortes, reduced the Parsua to vassalage and laid siege to the Assyrian capital of Nineveh. According to Herodotus, whose chronology here appears unlikely, the Median siege of Nineveh had to be drastically postponed. This time, unsure of his Scythian alliances, Cyaxares saw his rear menaced by a new Scythian invasion pouring into the Iranian plateau. Such were their shock tactics that, according to Herodotus, Cyaxares was forced for 28 years to buy them off with tribute. By 612 BC Cyaxares was in a position to capture Assyrian Nineveh and force his terms of peace on Babylon's Nabupolassar, who had joined the Medes against Nineveh in the final years of siege. Once he had defeated the Assyrian general Assuruballit at Harran, Cyaxares had won over all Mesopotamia, and after successive campaigns in Armenia, where the Urartian kingdom had been enfeebled by Scythian incursion, the whole arc of land from the Halys in the north to Susa in the south was his. Although Lydia on his Anatolian flank, and Chaldaea in the south of Mesopotamia remained unconquered, Cyaxares can truly be regarded as the builder of the Median empire, the first Iranian and nomadic empire the ancient Near East had known. The only rival lines claimant to the leadership of such an empire, those of Ariaramnes and his brother Cyrus, 'The Persians', remained in vassalage.

It was a marriage alliance between the daughter of Astyages, son and successor of Cyaxares as king of Media, and Cambyses, the son of Cyrus, 'King of Kings, King of Anshan' (albeit a vassal!) that produced a second Cyrus. In 559 BC Cyrus II became vassal king of Anshan and is named in the Babylonian Chronicle as king of Parsa from 547 onwards. He cultivated the military potentialities of the Persian tribesmen and, both to

Fig. 18

rival Ecbatana and show the vassal status of the Ariaramnes branch, whose territory either he or Cambyses I had conquered, built a new royal city in the territory of Fars. This was the first Achaemenid city, Pasargadae, built possibly in the territory of a tribe of that name and not necessarily connected with the tribal Parsua. Cyrus openly cast around for an ally against Media. A convenient and indeed willing ally was Nabonidus (Nabunaid), usurper of Nebuchadnezzar's throne.

As far as Nabonidus was concerned, an alliance with Cyrus was ordained by the gods. Leaving the rule of Babylon in the hands of Balshazzar (who plays so prominent a role in the book of Daniel), Nabonidus marched to Syria, whilst Cyrus engaged Astyages, who was a weakling hampered by the defection to Cyrus of his two best generals. The outcome was as predicted: Nabonidus conquered almost all lands west to the seaboard of Syria, whilst the Persians plundered Ecbatana and carried off its treasure to Pasargadae.

There were two reasons why the Babylonian-Achaemenid alliance could not withstand these victories. The first was that the close ethnic affinity between the Persians and the conquered Medes was bound to upset the new international balance: once they had conquered Media, the Persians found themselves in control of the Median empire, which included much Mesopotamian territory within Babylon's sphere. The second reason was Babylon's decline and Nabonidus' great interest in the conquest of Arabia, in which he had chosen to reside. It was inevitable, therefore, that Cyrus should before long swallow up Babylonia.

But this process took place piecemeal, for meanwhile trouble from a new quarter engaged the energies of Cyrus, although in the course of dealing with it he had to establish his hold on the Assyrian cities, Arbela, Nineveh and Assur. The new threat came from beyond the Halys, where Croesus of Lydia, upon the fall of the Median empire, was determined to recover his

Fig. 18. Sculptured genie on the door jamb of the Gatehouse (palace R) at Pasargadae. Height about $8\frac{1}{2}$ ft. (5, 6, 86)

former territories. The clash came in 547: with the whole of nothern Mesopotamia, north Syria and south-east Turkey consolidated behind Cyrus, Croesus was routed. His capital, Sardis, situated in difficult mountain territory, fell, and Croesus, the richest man on earth, immolated himself on a funeral pyre. The defeat of Croesus affected no people more than the Greeks. The new contacts between Persians and the Greek settlements of the Ionian coast formerly subjected to newly conquered Lydia have passed into the best-known chapter of world history.

Details of the division and downfall of the commercial and oracle-ridden Ionian Greek cities belong properly to Greek history; to the Persians they were *initially* a minor frontier problem. Certainly a faction in the Greek cities saw in submission to Persia the continuance of the commercial advantages they had enjoyed whilst belonging to the Lydian empire. One by one they either submitted or hatched abortive plans to evacuate their settlements to western Mediterranean sites. The indigenous Lycians, a remnant of the Luqqu 'Sea Raiders' who in the late second millennium had successfully harassed the Hittite empire and were now a largely agricultural people, shut themselves up in their city of Xanthus and fought to the death. Lycia, Lydia and Ionia were converted into separate provinces.

Nabonidus had entered an alliance with Croesus against the Persians; there was now a better case against him. Gradually Babylonian territory was whittled away, but there was no direct attack on Nabonidus. Instead, by a process of internal disintegration and the revolt of Babylonia's Elamite subjects in Susa, complete decline set in. Babylonia was no longer a threat: the governor of Susa, Gabaru, or Gobryas as he was known to the Greeks, defected to Cyrus in the summer of 546.

Six years were to elapse before Nabonidus was directly subjugated. Meanwhile in the north-central Iranian plateau and on the south-eastern side of the Caspian, the region loosely known as Varkana (Greek: Hyrcania), tribes were subdued. To the south lay the more powerful Parthians, whose king was forced to accept a satrapy. It was probably at this time that Cyrus overran the Aryan homelands of Margiana, Sogdiana and Choresmia, as far as the river Jaxartes (Sir-Darja) and attacked the Massagetai beyond it, although it is quite uncertain whether these eastern campaigns took place before his conquest of Babylon as Herodotus relates. Finally, in October 539, harassed by opposition at home to his religious policies and the discontent of foreign captives and businessmen in his capital, Nabonidus opened Babylon's gates to the Persian army without striking a defensive blow.

The conquest of Babylonia brought the Persians directly into the context of Biblical history. In Babylon itself, at Tel

Abib on the River Kabar, where Ezekiel lived, and at Nippur, south-east of Babylon, were colonies of exiles of whom there is either Biblical or (as at Nippur) archaeological record. To these the conquest of Cyrus came as a liberation. He was hailed as the servant of Yahweh, the anointed of Israel, and the praise heaped upon him by Second Isaiah has led many to believe in the possibility of the existence in Babylon of a pro-Persian Jewish plot. Gobryas was made the city's first Persian Governor.

Palestine and Syria had been finally made tributary to the Babylonian empire by the campaigns of Nebuchadnezzar in the closing years of the seventh century BC. After some few years of vassalage, the reigning king of Judah, Jehoiakim, expecting support from Egypt, grew bold enough to withhold the tribute due usually to Babylon. His successor, the weakling Zedekiah, had openly revolted and was finally reduced by Nebuchadnezzar's forces in 587 BC. Large numbers of influential Jews were deported into exile in Babylon where the outcome of Babylonian policies was keenly watched. One such observer, the prophet Daniel, graphically portrayed the portents of Babylon's fall in the story of the writing on the wall at Balshazzar's feast, foretelling the division of the empire at the hands of Medes and Persians under Cyrus.

Documentary evidence reveals Cyrus' attitude on matters of religion at least in Mesopotamia, where Nabonidus by his antiquarian interest in certain northern deities and his open favouritism and state patronage of chosen shrines had upset the balance of religious practices. Cyrus claims that by Marduk's command he 'resettled' all the gods of Sumer and Akkad whom Nabonidus had brought into Babylon by restoring their cult images to their rightful palaces and chapels, 'which made them happy'. Taken in conjunction with the Iranian nature of Cyrus' religious beliefs, which were ethical and universalistic rather than nationalistic and centred round particular shrines, these events form the background to his edict permitting the exiled Jews to return to Jerusalem.

Whilst there is no evidence of a general resettlement, the place which the restoration and rebuilding of the temple (albeit on a modest scale) occupies in the Old Testament distorts the picture of actual conditions in Palestine under Persian dominion. Judah was only one of the five provinces into which the region 'Beyond the River' was divided; the others were Syria (Athura), Megiddo, Samerina (Samaria of Israel), Ashdod in Philistia, Ammon in Transjordan.

The story of the conquest of Babylon by Cyrus is fully recorded in a Babylonian chronicle of the twentysecond year of Darius (500 BC), but a shorter document, the 'Cyrus cylinder' from Babylon, is a contemporary record by Cyrus himself. This tells of his restoration of temples and deported peoples and undoubtedly refers to the religious misbehaviour of Nabonidus when it speaks of the inappropriate rituals instituted at Ur, the city which, since earliest Sumerian times, had been associated with the moongod Nannar, and later with his Babylonian equivalent, Sin. Another clay cylinder of Cyrus found at Ur indicates that Cyrus restored Sin to his rightful shrine and as preparation for the god's return began in his first year the last building operations of which there is any trace at Ur. A gate on the northeast side of the sacred enclosure was renovated and fitted with new doors; Cyrus stamped his name on the new bricks surrounding the doorposts. Each inscription, like those on the longer documents, expressed the gratitude of Cyrus to the gods for having delivered these new lands to him, and it is this which prompted his restoration of shrines. He uses a simple stereotyped official formula, and such was in all probability the nature of his edict to the Jews.

Not as a conqueror or liberator did Cyrus intend to claim the loyalty of his Babylonian subjects but rather by giving his kingship constitutional grounds and establishing himself as benefactor of Marduk, the chief deity of Babylon. Helpfully, Nabonidus himself was no blood descendant of his predecessor Nebuchadnezzar and thus could in all truthfulness be represented as a usurper. Even whilst making allowances for the usual propaganda practised by Near Eastern conquerors, there can be little doubt that Cyrus' peaceful and benevolent conquest was something new in Mesopotamian history. The populace was neither decimated nor deported, the statues of the city's gods were not degraded; instead the religious, political and economic life of Babylon had joyous expectations of the new king.

In Babylon, Cyrus received the homage of the Syrian princes and returned to residence in Ecbatana by 537, his direct participation in Babylonian affairs over. As viceroy he left behind his eldest son Cambyses, who as early as 538 had taken his father's place in the Babylonian New Year festival. It is possible that in the following years Cyrus himself was occupied in carrying out the expeditions to eastern Iran and south-central Asia mentioned earlier, or at least in extending and consolidating his eastern empire. In wealth and culture the eastern provinces had little to give compared with Babylon, but the uniting of the Perso-Median peoples with their older and nearest kindred much enriched the cultural and spiritual resources of the Achaemenids. Especially in the Aryan provinces of central Asia the religious and social ideals of the Aryans had remained pure, and it is generally agreed that they favoured the rise, probably in Choresmia in Cyrus' time, of the great religious teacher Spitama Zarathustra (Zoroaster).

Whilst we can be certain that the river Jaxartes was regarded by Cyrus as the eastern limit of his conquests, we have no archaeological knowledge of any of the fortifications he built along it, including the city Kyreschata (Cyropolis) known to Classical writers. Beyond it the Massagetae, ethnically Aryans,

Fig. 19

did not submit to him, and it was in a battle against these 'fish-eaters', who according to Herodotus' semi-legendary account were ruled by queen Tomyris, that Cyrus lost his life in 530 BC, fallen victim, it is thought, to those outflanking swift cavalry tactics which the Persians were later to make a military speciality. His embalmed body was taken to Pasargadae where his tomb, a small aedicule on a stepped platform, built in Urartian fashion, is one of the principal monuments of Achaemenid Iran.

Some eight years before his death Cyrus installed his son, now a mature man, as king in Babylon. Cambyses is the only Achaemenid king whose career as a crown prince we are able to trace in contemporary administrative documents. Cyrus had already taken great pains to have Cambyses installed with the ceremony of approval by Marduk, and to the Babylonians he was their legitimate king, readily accepted.

With Palestine under Persian control, Egypt was to be the next target. Egypt had been allied to Croesus and her aid had been sought by Palestine: Polycrates of Samos, the chief instigator of Greek resistance to Persia, was allied to the pharaoh Amasis. The disaffection amongst the Egyptians caused by Amasis' misrule had brought influential exiles, both Egyptian and Greek, to the Persian court; valuable military information was at the disposal of Cambyses. The immediate cause of his invasion of Egypt is unknown, but was probably connected with Amasis' claim to Cyprus and the consequent danger of the disaffection of the Phoenician cities, whose economy was bound up with Egypt and Cyprus. Aided by the backing of the Phoenician fleet, which he had been careful to win over and which was a factor of new importance in Persian strategy, Cambyses marched to the Nile. Taking Sais and Memphis, the two royal cities, in 525/524 BC, he captured Psammetichus III, the pharaoh who meanwhile had succeeded Amasis. Eventually he penetrated up the Nile

Fig. 19. Tomb of Cyrus at Pasargadae. Height 36 ft. (87)

to the borders of the mysterious and dreaded Ethiopians. Egypt was formed into the satrapy of Mudraya, with Memphis as its capital. Foreign traders, transporters and shipbuilders soon flocked there; mercenaries, both Greek and Phoenician, were quartered in its substantial barracks. Once more, as in Ionia, Greek trading colonies were at Persian mercy: Daphnae and Naucratis in the Eastern Delta lands were in Persian hands, and soon the Greek Libyan foundations Cyrene and Barca offered submission.

It speaks well for the policies of Cambyses that Greek traders flocked to Egypt. Over his treatment of the Egyptians themselves we must preserve some impartiality, since the monstrous activities attributed to him by Herodotus, especially the disinterment and lashing of Amasis' corpse, are coloured by Greek propaganda and the information Herodotus picked up on his visit to Egypt just after Inarus had revolted against Achaemenid rule. At the same time the surviving records include the laudatory inscriptions of an official who probably played a crucial part in aiding the Persian conquest and was specially favoured by Cambyses. This was Udjahorresne, a man of astonishingly wide accomplishments, at least in officialdom. He had been commander of the fleet under Psammetichus and was now chief physician to Cambyses and a priest in the medical and theological school at Sais. On his hieroglyphic stela Udjahorresne tells how Cambyses invaded the country, how he recognised the importance of the Egyptian shrine at Udjahorresne's native Sais, how he restored the temple revenue and indeed visited the shrine and paid homage. It is made quite clear that the author had by his intervention saved the inhabitants of Sais from terrible troubles during the invasion and after it, and, reading between the lines, it is probable that this was due to his merits as captain of a fleet which had defected to the Persians. Not only the gratitude but also the achievement of Udjahorresne has special significance, since demotic documents suggest that royal endowment of Egyptain temples was greatly reduced by Cambyses, and the priests were left to provide the sacrificial grain and animals by their own efforts.

Encouraged by the success of his Babylonian enterprises, Cambyses was careful to adopt the titles of Egyptian royal protocol and to put himself in proper filial relationship to the Egyptian gods. In the hieroglyphic epitaph and sarcophagus provided by him for a dead sacred Apis bull interred in the Serapeum at Memphis, Cambyses takes the pharaonic titles 'King of Upper and Lower Egypt, Son of Ra, Endowed with All Life' and is pictured wearing pharaonic costume and kneeling before the Apis bull in an Egyptian posture of adoration.

By the standards of the ancient world, Egypt now belonged to Persia by right of conquest, but Cambyses himself appears to have legitimised his rule by other claims. His adoption of the Egyptian royal title 'Offspring of Ra', as well as his prostration before the statue of Neith at Sais, have been regarded by some scholars as formal acts implying legitimization and coronation. The absence of the Persian formula 'the great god [Ahuramazda] chose me' from the Achaemenid royal titles used in Egyptian inscriptions and the use by Cambyses and his successors of the title 'King of Egypt, King of Lands' in Egypt suggest that Cambyses was at pains to show claims to the

Builders of Empire

Egyptian throne independent of conquest. It now seems well established that Cambyses dated his rule over Egypt not from the date of his conquest but from the year 329/30, in which he ascended the Persian throne, and that he used both Persian and Egyptian systems of counting his regnal years. Thus, whereas Cambyses left Egypt in 522 B C, papyrus documents in Egyptian demotic dated to his eighth year may be taken as evidence that the Egyptians counted his years as King of Persia, not those of Egypt alone.

The reasons which may have justified Cambyses' claims are totally obscured by our lack of understanding of the treaty relationships existing between Egypt and the Babylonian empire to which Cyrus laid claim by his conquest of Babylon. Egypt lay open after Nebuchadnezzar had routed the Egyptians at Carchemish in 605 B C, yet neither Nebuchadnezzar nor his successor Nabonidus invaded it. Throughout their reigns, formal treaties in which Egypt accepted an inferior role must have governed the relations between the two countries. We have no records of such a treaty, but Nabonidus apparently claimed Egypt as an ally and there is the evidence of Herodotus of intermarriage at this point between the royal houses of the two countries.

Xenophon emphatically stated that Egypt and Cyprus were already claimed as tributary by Cyrus (*Cyropaedia* I. i. 4, VIII. vi. 20) and Greek stories claimed that Nitetis, the daughter of pharaoh Apries, had been married either to Cyrus or to Cambyses. If these stories are correct, they may possibly indicate the continuance and cementing of the terms of an earlier Egypto-Babylonian vassal treaty renewed between Cyrus and Apries who had been virtually deposed by Amasis in 569 and died in 566 B C. They might also indicate Cyrus' (or Cambyses') claim to Egypt by right of dowry after Apries' death in the same way as, according to Xenophon, Media had been obtained by Cyrus from Cyaxares as the dowry of Cyaxares' daughter Cassandane whom Cyrus married. Cyaxares had no son 'born in wedlock' and since Amasis was a usurper it is possible that the rightful successor was Cyrus. Was it for his usurpation of Cyrus' right by dowry that Cambyses took Amasis' corpse and whipped it? There are grounds for believ- ing that transmission of countries by dowry was recognised by Persian law. Since it was a practice so foreign to Greek law, it is unlikely that Herodotus and other Greek historians invented it, and it occurs again in Herodotus' account of Cyrus' last campaign, before which he is said to have sought a marriage with the queen of the Massagetae. She refused it, 'knowing that it was not herself he was wooing, but the kingdom of the Massagetae' (Herodotus Bk I, 205). But the historicity of such marriages and their dowry-rights is a different matter, and very great difficulties of chronology are found in some of the accounts of the intermarriages of Egyptian princesses with Babylonian and Achaemenid kings – even accepting the polygamy of the Babylonian and Persian rulers and the possibility of purely formal diplomatic marriages. Whatever the truth, the claim by dowry-right was good propaganda, and had the desired effect at least on the Greeks.

The incorporation of Cyprus in the Achaemenid empire presumably followed the invasion of Egypt. The Cypriote cities founded by Phoenicia, especially Citium, could perhaps have been claimed by right of the incorporation of the mother country, but we do not in fact know the constitutional rela- tionship between Tyre and her colonies or whether indeed Cyprus had been claimed by the Babylonians. The Greek historian Diodorus speaks of conquest of Cyprus by Apries about 570 BC, but in Herodotus (Bk II, 182) this conquest is attributed to Amasis. Certainly it seems that Cyprus was not incorporated in the empire before the conquest of Egypt, and the references in Greek literature to Cyrus' claim to it might have resulted from propaganda in Cambyses' reign.

Cambyses has often been presented as an unworthy heir to the greatness of Cyrus. Whilst we cannot accept him as the epileptic lunatic described by Herodotus, it may be that he neither possessed his predecessor's ability in the field nor enjoyed his loyal following at home. Fortune and history have dealt unkindly with him, but we must remember that his invasion of Egypt was no mean achievement, and in his use of the Phoenician navy, without which Cyprus could not have been held, Cambyses brought about the Persian dominance at sea which was soon to prove indispensable in controlling the coastal regions of Asia Minor and extending Persian conquest into Europe.

CHAPTER IV

The Great Kings

WHATEVER THE CIRCUMSTANCES of his accession to the Persian throne, it seems certain that Darayavaush, Darius I, had something to hide. The accounts of Herodotus and Darius of the events following the death of Cambyses, whilst differing in most details, both agree that Darius took the throne from the hands of an impostor, a Magus named Gau-mata who claimed to be Bardiya (called Smerdis by Herodotus), the brother of Cambyses, whom the king had secretly murdered. Herodotus points out that the degree of physical likeness of this man to the dead Smerdis deceived even his own mother and makes his seizure of power in Media the cause for the sudden return of Cambyses from Egypt. Both accounts agree that the real Smerdis had been secretly murdered by Cambyses, Darius placing the murder before, Herodotus during the Egyptian expedition. In either case no great amount of time elapsed between Cambyses' death and the appearance of Gaumata-Smerdis, to whom, for unstated reasons, the whole population of the central Achaemenid provinces gave their support. There was, according to Darius, a danger that a purge carried out by Gaumata would erase the true Bardiya from human memory. No one dared to oppose this terror except Darius, who conquered Gaumata and his followers at the Median city of Sikajavati.

The entire situation seems most unlikely. Why was so important a personage as the king's brother, who according to Herodotus accompanied Cambyses to Egypt, so soon for-gotten whilst an unknown impostor readily obtained the following of most of the empire? Herodotus tries to make it more plausible by placing Gaumata's appearance immediately after the secret murder of Smerdis, but the rock inscription of

Behistun in which Darius recorded his rise to power places the murder three years earlier. Is it possible, one wonders, that the man Darius slew and who gained such a following was no impostor but was in fact the true Bardiya? Could not Gaumata be an invention of official court history which deceived Herodotus? Traditions used by Xenophon and the playright Aeschylus know nothing of an impostor but alike preserve the existence of legitimate successors descended from Cambyses. The entire circumstances of Darius' accession and first regnal year certainly do not suggest that he acquired the throne amidst the acclaim of a people smarting from the terrors of Gaumata's brief reign. Between the lines of Darius' successful progaganda his unlawful usurpation following internal rivalry in the house of Achaemenes appears to lie hidden, though not proven.

By descent Darius was son of Hystaspes, grandson of Arsames, great-great-grandson(?) of that Ariaramnes whom Cyaxares the Mede had subjected. Hystaspes – Arsames probably also – was satrap of Parthia, and the whole line had probably viewed with some envy the successful rise of Ariaramnes' brother Cyrus I of the parallel branch of the Achaemenid family against their common vassalage imposed by Median Astyages. Moreover, whilst Cyrus by intermarriage with the house of Cyaxares' family acquired much Median blood, the Ariaramnes line besides being the elder had remained purely Persian. It is possible that, with Cambyses abroad in Egypt, the descendants of Ariaramnes seized their chances of reasserting the line. Only Bardiya, son of Cyrus the Great, stood in Darius' way, and if it was indeed Bardiya himself whom Darius conquered, by representing him as an impostor, Darius not only legitimised his title to the throne but also made sure that the Cyrus line lost all right of succession. This was not the only occasion on which Darius was to use the weapon of declaring rivals illegitimate to suit his political ends. With both his father and grandfather still alive, however, he claimed the throne by personal ambition rather than immediate right of succession. He had been close to Cambyses, according to Herodotus, and had accompanied him as adjutant in Egypt. He must have left the Persian army in Palestine to hurry home and press his claim. Implicit in the story is a definite rivalry between Medes and Persians still active in the government of the empire. Cyrus was strictly a 'Median' king; it was from the throne of Media at Ecbatana that he chose to rule. Gaumata is presented as a Magus, a member of the specifically Median priestly caste, and it is possible that Cambyses' brother was indeed a Magus. It was in a Median city that Gaumata was conquered. All this appears to be stressed by Darius. His claim to have restored the religious shrines destroyed by Gaumata is certain evidence for a difference in religious affiliation between the Persians and the rival Median party; whilst in the Behistun inscription he is at pains to stress his own Persian descent. Cyrus' reign is not mentioned, and of Cambyses only that little is told which implies his unfitness to rule because of his treatment of his brother and the complete vacancy of the throne caused by the latter's death. The real purpose of Darius is to discredit the Median dynasty and prove his right of succession. Since, as we have pointed out, dowry-right appears to have played some part in Achaemenid royal succession, Darius' subsequent marriages, first to two daughters of Cyrus II, Atossa and Artystone, and then to Phaedyme, daughter of one of 'The Seven', certainly appear as part of an effort at legitimisation, especially as two of these ladies had been married to Cambyses.

By right of conquest Darius was king. Either because of the division of allegiances over Bardiya or because the internal situation had provided an opportunity for revolt, the empire of Cyrus was completely broken. Only Bactria and Arachosia declared positively for Darius. Relying on the same six faithful followers who had assisted his fight against Bardiya and whose names he immortalised in the Behistun inscription, and trusting to his own genius as a general, Darius subdued the remaining territories in a little over a year. Almost all had revolted from Darius: Parsa, Media, Assyria, Parthia, Egypt, Margiana, the Sattagydia land and the Sakae. In eastern Parsa arose Vahyazdata who declared himself to be the murdered Bardiya! The revolt reached Bactria, and Parthia and Hyrcania, both of which were in the satrapy of Hystaspes, his father, declared against Darius. Armenia rose in support of Babylon. In Media a serious bid was made to revive the Median kingship by Phraortes, a descendant of Cyaxares, who now declared himself Khshathrita (the Median royal title?). Ecbatana went over to him and soon Armenia became an ally, whilst Parthia and Hyrcania were invaded and forced to submit.

In December 522, Darius found himself with nothing but the immediate territory of Babylon under military occupation, for even the throne of the central province of Parsa was firmly held by Vahyazdata, whose legitimacy had been recognised by the officers of the royal palace at Pasargadae. His campaigns against Armenia, Phraortes and Vahyazdata during the winter of 520/521 were only partially successful. In April 521 two of Darius' armies took the field: his general Artavardiya marched against Vahyazdata, whilst the king himself moved against Phraortes, whose army awaited Darius at Kampanda. The battle took place at Kunduru on May 7. Phraortes escaped to Raga (Rhages), was captured there and hanged in Ecbatana. Kunduru was the decisive battle for Darius and he chose the rocks at Behistun overlooking the plains of his victory as the site for his official monument.

Fig. 20

Thus by lightning strategy and the solidarity of his generals, aided also by the inability of his opponents to combine their interests and forces against him, Darius by the end of 521 held all Cyrus' former territories except Asia Minor and Egypt. Above the trilingual inscription, cut in bold relief, stands Darius accompanied by his bow- and spear-bearers. His right

Fig. 20

foot rests upon the prostrate figure of Gaumata, who stretches out both his hands in a gesture of submission. The left hand of Darius rests upon his standing bow; his right is raised in prayer towards the winged circlet of Ahuramazda who hovers above the scene holding out the coronation wreath in his left hand and raising the right in blessing. Behind Gaumata's supine figure stand nine captive rebel leaders, roped together by the neck and each with his hands fettered behind his back, and an accompanying label of his name and offences. Beneath the inscription the rock surface was cut vertically to prevent access and this is one reason why the inscription, especially the Persian and Elamite versions, has been remarkably well preserved. According to the Greek historian Ctesias, who visited the site about a century after the inscription was carved, a considerable area in front of the rock face was originally laid out as a park.

Besides presenting the official autobiography of the king, copies of which were doubtless made in more perishable materials and circulated round the empire, the Behistun inscription gives the earliest list of the satrapies into which the empire was divided. They are placed in a rough cyclic geo-

Fig. 21

graphical order beginning with the central provinces: Parsa, Khuvja (Elam); Babairush (Babylon, to which Palestine and Syria belonged); Athura (Assyria); Arabaya (the north-eastern portion of Arabia); Mudraya (Egypt); Tyaiy drayahya (the 'sea lands' on the northern coast of Asia Minor, administered from Dascylium); Sparda (Sardis and Lydia); Yauna (Ionia, the Greek settlements on the west coast of Asia Minor); Mada (Media); Armina (Armenia); Katpatuka (Cappadocia); Parthava (Parthia); Zranka (Drangiana, the area about Lake Hilmend); Haraiva (Areia, the region of modern Herat); Khuvarazmish (Choresmia, round modern Chiva); Bakhtrish (Bactria, on the upper course of the Oxus); Sugda (Sogdia, the region around modern Samarkand); Gandara (N. Punjab);

Fig. 20. King Darius victorious over Gaumata and the nine rebel leaders. Rock relief of Behistun (73)

Saka (the steppe-lands east of Bactria inhabited by Sakae); Thatagush (Sattagydia west of Gandara and south of Bactria); Harakhuvatish (Arachosia, south of Thatagush, Baluchistan); Maka (Oman and Muskat).

To provide the security of his move against Egypt, Darius settled the affairs of Judaea. Not all the exiled Jews had taken advantage of the permission granted by Cyrus in 538 for their return to Palestine. Amongst those left in Babylon was the prophet Ezra, and it is from his book that we can gather the unsatisfactory progress of the re-establishment of the Jewish state. The foundation stones of the second temple had been laid, and it appears that money and material were on hand for its completion. Work was however at a standstill, and although we are nowhere given the precise cause, it is probable that opposition to the new Jewish state from the Transjordanian Ammonites and from the Arabians and Edomites in the south weighed heavy at the Persian court. Either late in Cyrus' reign or early in that of Cambyses, the accession to the governorship of Judah of a Jew, Zerubbabel, grandson of Jehoiachin, last king of Judah, despite his pro-Babylonian name – 'seed of Babel' – brought a new nationalistic upsurge and a hope of re-establishing the Davidic monarchy. Palestine had little cause for complaint where Persian overlordship was concerned, and she did not throw in her lot with Babylon's revolt, since the new nationalism of Judah had a primarily religious motivation. The terms in which the prophet Haggai spoke remind us that the Jerusalem temple was conceived as the actual dwelling of Yahweh – 'must you dwell in panelled houses whilst this house is in ruins?' Certainly the Samaritans who dwelt around the Persian administrative centre at Samaria cannot have agreed to such a notion and this might have been another reason for delay in implementing the edict of Cyrus. Under Zerubbabel and the high priest Joshua, however, the Samaritans offered aid. It was the strict monotheist Haggai who opposed this pollution. Tattenai, the governor of 'Beyond the River', who was responsible now to Hystanes in Babylon, warned Darius of the way in which groups of zealots were urging Zerubabbel's independent kingship. Tattenai suddenly appeared on the scene in Jerusalem demanding to know who gave permission for the temple restoration. Consternation was caused when the Jews replied that not only had Cyrus given his permission in a special edict but also Sheshbazzar, the governor of Judah appointed by Cyrus, had laid the foundations. Tattenai was incredulous, and a stiff report to the chancellery began a search of the archives. In the library at Ecbatana the document drawn up by Cyrus was found; Darius, whose hold on the empire was still insecure, could not afford to ignore it.

Although Cambyses' hold appeared well consolidated, Egypt revolted, according to the Behistun inscription, while Darius was fighting the Babylonian pretender Nebuchadnezzar III. It is doubtful if the wording of the inscription implies a fully-fledged revolt; Darius' expedition to Egypt appears to have been primarily a show of strength, but amongst others it overawed the Greek colonists at Cyrene, whose territory was made into a new satrapy of Libya. It appears that from the beginning Darius found a ready accomplice in Udjahorresne, the former ally of Cambyses. This man, who had become one of Darius' staff at Susa, was sent back to Egypt to spread pro-Persian propaganda and to re-establish the medical school at Sais, where his stela (see page 60) was erected. The date of Darius' entry into Memphis can be calculated with certainty since it coincided with a period of mourning for the dead Apis bull. Darius seized the opportunity of endearing himself to the Egyptian people by offering a reward to the person who discovered the new-born bull calf which was believed to be the Apis reincarnation, and himself dedicated the epitaph of the deceased bull on August 31, 518. His activities in the country were much concerned with religion. Besides the restoration of the priestly school at Sais under Udjahorresne, in whose inscription Darius acknowledges himself the son of Neith, hieroglyphic inscriptions credit him with the construction of temples to Amon Ra in the Khargeh oasis and other temples at Edfu, Busiris and Elkab.

Two other significant activities of Darius are documented in Egypt: the digging of the 'Suez' canal and the codification of Egyptian Law as part of an aim to give the Empire a consistent legal system.

Darius was not the first to undertake the digging of a canal linking the Red Sea from near Bubastis through lake Timsah and the Wadi Toumilat to the Mediterranean. The canal had almost been completed under the pharaoh Necho, but Darius sent ships to reconnoitre it and found that it was dry along 85 km. of its length. The terminology of four of the surviving stelae erected by Darius along the course of the canal, one of which was discovered by de Lesseps whilst the modern canal was being dug in 1866, leave no doubt that it was a project

Fig. 22

Fig. 21. The satrapies of the Persian empire early in the reign of Darius I. Bracketed

CASPIAN SEA

(SAKA TIGRAKHAUDA)

KHUVARAZMISH

SAKA
(SAKA HAUMAVARGA)

SUGDA

BAKHTRISH

ADA

PARTHAVA

HARAIVA

GANDARA

ZRANKA

Karun

Pasargadae
•←Persepolis

PARSA

THATAGUSH

R.Indus

HARAKHUVATISH

(HINDUSH)

MAKA

0 ——— 500
Scale of Miles

names indicate satrapies formed under Xerxes or late in Darius' reign

73

which interested him personally. Its digging seems to have been closely connected with his visit to Egypt in 518 and the immediate consequences, the sending of 44 tribute ships to Egypt by the canal route and the commissioning of the Greek Skylax of Caryanda to explore the shore of the Arabian Gulf as far as India in a methodical manner, seem already to imply preparations for the augmenting of the Indian territories which Darius undertook in 515, extending Thatagush south-eastwards to the Indus to form a new province of Hindush.

Meanwhile the provinces of Asia Minor had remained untouched. Already under Cambyses, Oroites, the satrap of Sparda, had acquired an unparalleled degree of autonomy. He conducted his own foreign policy, which included appro-priating the lands of Ionia's most powerful tyrant, Polycrates of Samos, and had remained totally aloof in the wars between Darius and Media, using them as an opportunity not only to further his independence but to gain control of the Ionian satrapy by the murder of the satrap Mitrobates in Dascylium. His contempt for Darius' pleas for submission may have been due to his knowledge of the Great King's military commit-ments now that Egypt was occupied. We cannot tell at what stage Darius decided to settle the Oroites affair, but he appar-ently managed it without drawing on his troops. He sent Bagaios, one of his trusted generals, to Sardis to stir the Persian garrison there to mutiny. In the course of it, Oroites was assassinated.

Thereafter throughout the reign of Darius the military affairs of the empire were centred on Ionia and Persian history became Greek history, seen through Greek eyes and written from the standpoint of Greek interests. It has often been suggested that 'the trouble between the Greeks and the Persians', which were of crucial significance for western civilisation and which gave birth to the objective recording of history by Thucydides, were but a minor irritation on the western extremity of Persia's

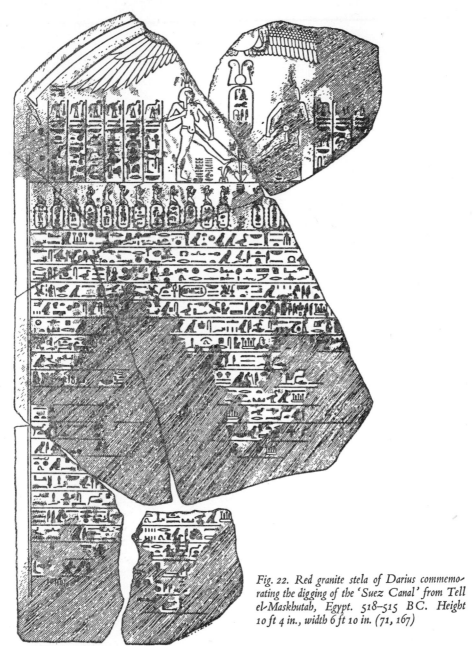

Fig. 22. Red granite stela of Darius commemo-
rating the digging of the 'Suez Canal' from Tell
el-Maskhutah, Egypt. 518–515 BC. Height
10 ft 4 in., width 6 ft 10 in. (71, 167)

policies. This is far from the truth. In dealing with Ionia, Persia became increasingly aware of the existence of the Greek motherland, her political and economic *koine* and wide trade interests. Never before had Persia come to grips with a maritime power. Her own navy, conscripted from Cyprus and Phoenicia, was an arm difficult to control. Because of the nervous state of Ionia, the satrapy of Lydia was of the greatest importance and Darius appointed to it his brother Artaphernes.

Apart from Ionia, the value of the Greek cities on the west and north coasts of the Black Sea was well appreciated by Darius. These cities, founded mostly as daughter colonies of Miletus, long subject to Persia, were the granaries of the Ionian and mainland Greek cities alike. Darius was anxious to explore European territory, especially the lands of the western Scyths in the present-day regions of European Turkey and Rumania. After leaving Susa with his army in 513, he was supported by a large Ionian Greek fleet which sailed from Ionia to the mouth of the Ister. Crossing the Bosphorus on a pontoon bridge of moored boats, Darius subdued the coast of Thrace and Getae in the hinterland and then moved northward into the territory about the Danube, which he crossed on a bridge constructed by the sappers of the Greek fleet. Beyond the Danube was Scythian territory, and here Darius' army was at the same disadvantage as had been that of Cyrus among the Massagetae. Avoiding head-on battle, the Scyths harassed the Persian troops with light cavalry skirmishes and quickly disappeared beyond reach into the deserted landscape. Throughout this operation, the rear of Darius' army was exposed to Ionian defection. But Histiaeus, tyrant of Miletus, was tardy to strike a blow; on his retreat, Darius found the Danube bridge intact and was able to return eventually to Asia Minor. He left part of his army in Europe under the command of Megabazus, satrap of Dascylium. Megabazus completed the conquest of Thrace and brought Amyntas, king of Macedonia, to acknowledge the sovereignty of the Great King. The Ionian region was placed under a new satrap, Otanes, resident at Byzantium in order to gain control of the Bosphorus traffic. It was not to be expected that the Ionian cities, favoured though many of them were, would for long tolerate being severed from their Black Sea colonies and that the mainland cities would view with unconcern the movement of Otanes and Megabazus into the north of peninsular Greece.

It was the internal political situation in Athens which brought matters to a head. In order to preserve her experiments in democracy under Cleisthenes from Spartan encroachment, Athens first sent tokens of submission to Artaphernes at Sardis in 510; but Persia was persuaded that it was more in her interests to restore to Athens the tyrant Hippias, previously expelled and now resident at the Persian court. Though Cleisthenes himself had meanwhile been expelled from Athens, Athenian fear of the restoration of Hippias overrode all traditional enmity toward Sparta. Athens was prepared to fight. Whilst this threat was hanging over the mother city, the Ionian colonists became increasingly dissatisfied with the tyrants the Persian regime had foisted on them and with their loss of trade advantages resulting from the Persian hold on the Bosphorus. Miletus was the centre of disaffection, and its former tyrant, Histiaeus, whose mischief-making the Persians considered better controlled by exile in far-away Susa, now began to urge the reigning tyrant, Aristagoras, his son-in-law, to open revolt. Though Sparta possessed the military strength, the position at home of Cleomenes, the Spartan king, was weak, and he could no longer be certain of commanding against Persia the other members of his Peloponnesian alliance, particularly Corinth and Aegina, whose navies would be essential in any operation. Athens and Eretria together sent a contingent aboard twenty-five ships, which together with those of Miletus and other Ionian colonies conveyed the troops to Ephesus. The Greek allies marched on Sardis and burnt it; but they were unable to capture Arta-phernes and his garrison inside the citadel and were forced to retreat. As the Greeks marched back to the coast the Persian garrison made a sortie and attacked their rear, inflicting heavy loss. Athens withdrew from the fray, but this was offset by the Hellespontine cities and Cyprus throwing in their lot with the Greeks. As was usual in the Greek world, however, the cities of Cyprus were divided in their espousal of the Ionian cause and soon all fell to a Persian invasion. An expeditionary force, after capturing five rebel Hellespontine cities, invaded and subdued Caria. By these losses the revolt was doomed: Miletus could now be crushed. It was a pathetically inade-quate force which the rebels could now muster; depleted by loss and defection, only 353 triremes could be mobilised off Lade in the Milesian gulf against the united Phoenician, Cypriote, Egyptian and Cilician fleets. The inevitable Persian victory put an end to effective Ionian sea resistance. Soon Miletus was taken and burned, the Milesians being either slain or deported. The islands of Chios, Lesbos, Tenedos and the remaining rebel cities on the mainland suffered much the same fate.

The burning of Sardis by the Athenians was not forgotten, and when it became clear that neither Athens nor Sparta would follow Aegina and other states in submitting to the Persian overtures, or be impressed by Persia's encouragement of democratic regimes in the newly organised Ionian satrapy, Mardonius began the land invasion of peninsular Greece.

The enterprise miscarried. Although Mardonius announced his intention of taking Athens and Eretria, there were unfami-liar seas and unfriendly peoples still to be reckoned with. The great fleet which was supporting the land advance of the army was half wrecked in a storm off Mount Athos, and almost simultaneously Mardonius' army was defeated by the Macedonian Phrygians. A new army was mustered in Cilicia in 490, and under Datis the Mede and Artaphernes, a cousin of the crown prince Xerxes, was mounted on the troop carriers of the reorganised Persian navy and transported across the Aegean by way of Samos, Delos and Naxos. It captured Eretria in Euboea, Athens' close friend and trade ally. Since there were elements in Athens expectedly pro-Persian, especially the pro-Hippias faction and the democratic Alcmaeo-nidae, Datis might well have hoped that Athens would be handed over by treachery. But the Persians had been their own worst enemy: contrary to their normal policy, they had destroyed the temples and shrines of Eretria, and the fear caused to the artisans and the traders of the demos of Athens by the news of the burning and enslavement of Eretria by Datis overrode all factional and political opportunism. Thus when the Persian forces crossed the straits of Euboea and landed on the plain of Marathon on Hippias' advice, the whole Athenian army was drawn up to meet them. The outcome is one of the better-known events in history.

News of the Persian defeat at Marathon did not discourage the Great King. Throughout the next four years Darius laid plans for a greater invasion of Greece. In November of 486, however, he died in Persepolis at the age of sixty-four. We depend entirely on Herodotus for personal details of his life. In his effigy on the Behistun relief he is shown as a majestic but stocky figure. It appears from the Persepolis treasury tablets that he had a daughter of the same name as his best-loved wife, Artystone, for a tablet preserves a decree of Darius of 506 BC endowing her with a hundred sheep. Already within his life-time he had made for himself a rock-cut tomb in the rocky outcrop at Naqsh-i Rustam in the north-west of the plain in which stood his royal city, Persepolis. The frontage of the tomb is designed in three superimposed panels, the central one constituting the arcaded façade containing the tomb

Fig. 23

Plate 76

Fig. 23. Sculptured head of Darius I from the rock relief of Behistun (73)

entrance. In the panel above this is a huge throne-like dais supported by thirty miniature inhabitants of the satrapies. Upon this stands Darius, bow in hand, and in an attitude of adoration to the winged circlet of Ahuramazda which flies above him, as in the Behistun rock carving. Before the figure of the king stands a fire-altar. The trilingual text accompanying the Darius figure has caused considerable interest. Not only is it impressive in its own right as a declaration of Darius' high moral aspirations but the prevailing dualism of its expression and its specific terminology have led to its being recognised by a number of scholars as a quotation from one of the Avestan *gathas* and a proof that Darius was a Zoroastrian.

Several years before his death, Darius had settled the succession on his son by Atossa the daughter of Cyrus and sister of Cambyses. His name was Khshyarsha, Xerxes to the Greeks. Since he was born during Darius' kingship he was given precedence over his elder half-brother Artobazanes, by Darius' former marriage. Already in 498 Xerxes was named as crown prince and viceroy of Babylon. He was thirty-two when he came to the Persian throne.

Xerxes had neither the military ability nor the statecraft of his predecessors. Early in his reign his solutions to the unrest in Egypt and Babylon show the turn of tide in Achaemenid fortunes. After restoring the situation in Egypt he made it into an ordinary satrapy and no longer took to himself the rank and title of the Egyptian throne as had Cyrus and Darius. He appeared in Egypt as king of Persia. In Babylon too he insulted the city by placing the titles of his Babylonian kingship after those of Media and Persia; the days of 'taking the hands of Marduk' were past. But even so, the Babylonian title was short-lived. In 482 the satrap Zopyrus of Babylon was murdered and a Babylonian usurper, Bel-shimanni, took his place. Xerxes sent against him his best general, his son-in-law Megabyzus, and Babylon was soon taken. Xerxes dealt savagely with the city. Its walls and the Esagila temple built by Nebuchadnezzar were destroyed, and the great statue of Marduk, cast from twelve talents of pure gold, was taken away and melted down. Those who complained were liquidated. The estates of rich burghers were confiscated and distributed amongst the Persian nobility. Babylon would never rise again; she became an appendage to the satrapy of Assyria and her Palestinian and Syrian dependencies created into yet another satrapy. Thus did Xerxes deal with the two chief political components of the empire outside Media and Pars itself.

In 481, Xerxes took up temporary residence in Sardis in order to prepare a final invasion of Greece. Almost all the resources of the Achaemenid empire were mustered, and the description given by Herodotus (Bk VII, 56–99) of the foreign regiments making up Xerxes' vast army is one of the most valuable ethnographic documents of antiquity. Whilst the number of Xerxes' troops appears to be greatly exaggerated by Herodotus, there is no doubt that the land army was huge and well equipped. The Phoenician navy was the kernel of the sea force, and Herodotus' figure of more than 1,200 ships is confirmed by Aeschylus, who himself fought at Salamis.

Xerxes' intention of crushing Greece by sheer force showed the Persian ignorance not only of the sea and land conditions of that country but also of the factors of morale operative in the life of the Greek city states. Thermopylae and Salamis are sacred names in the history of western civilisation. The defence of the pass of Thermopylae by Leonidas and the three hundred Spartans was a tribute to Greek bravery; the sea victory at Salamis, on September 22, 480, in which half the Persian naval force was lost, although owing much to chance, was a tribute to Greek intelligence and an enormous boost to Greek morale. Xerxes had himself watched the battle and witnessed the deaths of several Persian notables. In the summer of 479, the Greeks routed the army of Mardonius at Plataea and killed Mardonius himself. The Persian forces in Greece were still far from broken by these Greek victories, but the Greeks were quick to strike a blow at the heart of the Persian military machine. Landing on the headland of Mycale north of Miletus a united Greek force defeated the Persian third army under Tigranes. The defeat of a second major Persian land force, and that on Xerxes' own territory, was indeed catastrophic enough, but the blow was aimed deeper. Without the support of the Ionians, Persian operations by both land and sea were difficult; without the Ionian fleet, which after Salamis was the mainstay of the Persian sea forces, they were impossible. After Mycale the leading Ionian states went over to Greece, and Persian hold on Ionia and the Hellespont was broken. The united Ionian fleets swept on to another great sea victory in the River Eurymedon in 566.

For Xerxes, Salamis was a personal tragedy. He had relied upon a show of strength to overawe the Greeks, and the way he is said to have reacted to failure by executing the Phoenician admiral, thereby alienating his most valuable Phoenician allies, shows a weakness and lack of intelligence in his character. After the defeat, he retired to Persepolis and, as far as we know, never left Persia again. A greater man would not have failed to realise that the vast territories won by conquest could not be held or infinitely extended in a monolithic system.

CHAPTER V

Palaces and Archives

WHEN CYRUS KING OF ANSHAN had taken posses-
sion of the Parsa lands, he constructed a dynastic
capital in the heart of the conquered territory. Its name,
Pasargadae (or Parsagadae), was interpreted by the Greeks as
'The Persian Camp', for unlike the other capitals and royal
cities of the ancient Near East it was not a city but was laid
out in sparsely inhabited land after the style of a military camp.
On the western bank of the river Pulvar, in a flat plain surrounded by low rolling hills, Cyrus marked off an extensive
walled park or 'Paradise' and erected scattered buildings
(originally set among trees) and a fort. It was entered on the
south through a monumental gatehouse with its entrance
guarded by two huge granite winged bulls of Assyrian style
and backed by a pair of human-headed bulls on the inside.
The gatehouse itself, known also as 'palace R', is a small
rectangular building with porticos and small chambers on all
four sides. On one of the orthostatic doorways which give
access to these is carved what is perhaps the earliest surviving
piece of Achaemenid sculpture, a four-winged human genie *Fig. 18*
wearing a Syrian robe and an Egyptian crown, a combination
which most probably indicates a Phoenician iconographic
source. The simple inscription accompanying the figure,
'I, Cyrus, the King, the Achaemenid', is the only known type
of inscription of Cyrus the Great. It is repeated on two other
buildings standing a few hundred yards to the north of the
gatehouse and known as palaces S and P.

Palace S, also known as the Audience Hall, consists of a
rectangular chamber with a portico of double columns on
all four sides. On the southern side the portico is flanked by
two square towers which adjoin the corners of the main hall;

but on the northern side the portico is flanked by antae formed by projections of the main wall of the building. The roof of the rectangular audience hall was supported by two rows of four columns down the centre. Although the walls survive in ground-plan only, the height of the columns has been cal- culated to show that the central hall stood several feet higher than the eighteen feet of the surrounding portico and that in all probability therefore the building was lit by clerestory openings. The columns had unfluted shafts of white stone with capitals and bases in contrasting black. The bases had a plain discoid torus on a square plinth and the capitals were in the shape of addorsed bulls, lions and horses and introduce us to this distinctive feature of Achaemenid architecture. Sculp- tured panels adorned the doorways placed in the centre of each of the four walls but only the lower portions of these have survived. One appears to have depicted three bare-footed priests leading a sacrificial ox, but the eastern and western doorways had reliefs of what appear to be composite quad- rupeds. At least, it is possible to reconstruct the relief of the eastern doorway as a monster consisting of the foreparts of a man and fish and the hind parts of a bull, reminiscent of a Median theme found in Scythia (p. 138). Palace P (250 × 140 ft) seems to have been designed as a residence and is a longer rectangular building divided into four rooms, of which the largest is a central columned hall with thirty closely-set wooden columns on stone bases. Columned porticos 20 feet high ran the length of the longest sides. The two black limestone door- ways leading from the central chamber into the two porticos were decorated with reliefs of Cyrus leaving the chamber accompanied by his parasol-bearer. Both the theme and the treatment differ little from the figure of Darius leaving the audience chamber at Persepolis, but regrettably the upper portion of the sculptures is fragmentary and comparison is limited to robes and feet. There is clear indication that many details of the sculpture were overlaid with gold foil and the identity of the royal figure as that of Cyrus is assured by a short inscription on a portion of the robe. The formula of this inscription, 'Cyrus, the Great King, the Achaemenid', has been taken by Olmstead to indicate that the building was erected by Cyrus after the defeat of Astyages, hence the title 'Great King', and that the simpler inscription 'I, Cyrus, the King, the Achaemenid' inscribed on palaces R and S and in an anta of palace P itself indicates structures erected whilst Cyrus was still a vassal king of Anshan under the Medes. The absence of the personal pronoun from the garment inscription coupled with the style of the relief has led Frankfort to suggest that the reliefs of Cyrus were the work of Darius and to follow Erdmann's hypothesis that since the Cyrus relief was accompanied by a much damaged trilingual inscription including a Babylonian version, it must at least post-date the conquest of Babylon in 539. All these suggestions with their implications for dating the emergence of a distinctive style of Achaemenid sculpture must be treated with caution. Against the argument of Olmstead, must be set the consideration that Cyrus is unlikely to have been able to build a capital outside Anshanite territory, while still a vassal of the Medes. Against Frankfort, it must be pointed out that the Cyrus inscriptions of all three Pasargadae palaces were trilingual, even that formerly accompanying the genie relief, which he places earliest. No other building activities of Darius at Pasargadae are known, nor does it seem politically likely that this monarch would glorify Cyrus. The argument also leaves out of account the style of the sculptures in palace S.

Much of our knowledge of Pasargadae we owe to the work of Ernst Herzfeld and to the aerial and surface surveys conducted by the University of Chicago in the 1930's. These latter reveal that a great amount of excavation work remains to be done at the site particularly with regard to the tower and fortified area to the north of the residential palaces. It is hoped that a team of British archaeologists now working at the site will make further discoveries of value. Under Darius, the foundations were laid for the most splendid of the Achaemenid architectural achieve-ments and during his reign not only was Persepolis begun but new palaces in Persepolis style were built in Susa and Babylon.

The city plan of Babylon laid down by Nebuchadnezzar's building activities was left substantially unaltered during the Persian period. His summer palace seems to have remained standing until Alexander's time; but a new palace for the crown prince Xerxes was begun by Darius in 498 BC, since a business tablet dated to Darius' twenty-fourth year deals with a delivery of material for building it. The excavation in the southern part of Nebuchadnezzar's city at Babylon un-covered a fragmentary stone plinth bearing the name of Darius together with fragments of bell-shaped column bases com-parable to those of Persepolis and units of glazed-brick friezes which picture portions of the weapons and dress of the Elamite Persian guards, repeated on a larger scale at Susa. But this 'Persian Building' was too ruined for us to tell exactly how it looked, although it does appear to have been an *apadana* or columned hall. We cannot on the fragmentary inscriptional evidence ascribe the building to Darius I, let alone identify it as the 'house of the King's son' referred to in the tablet. Further evidence for the activities of Darius in the city is the discovery in the ruins of Nebuchadnezzar's old palace museum of a stone bearing a Babylonian transcript of part of Darius' Behistun inscription and the large number of Babylonian business documents dated to the time of Darius, which were perhaps scattered from the 'house of archives where the treasures were laid up in Babylon' (Ezra 6, 1). An inscription of 'Artaxerxes son of Darius II' from the 'Persian Building' ruins is one of many both historical and archaeological showing that Babylon was the royal residence for subsequent monarchs for a part of each year. Ctesias, the Greek physician of Artaxerxes II, has left a valuable account of the splendid glazed tile-work of the walls of Babylon in his day and it may well be that where he comes to describe a hunting scene he is referring to the circuit wall of the southern citadel on which the 'Persian Building' stood.

The buildings and decorative techniques learned by Darius in Babylon were transferred to the Elamite capital of Susa, an ancient city dating back to early Bronze Age times and the focal point of wealthy trade-routes coming up from the Persian Gulf. In Elamite times a mound had grown up on the eastern side of this earliest nodus of settlement and this became the site of the palace of Darius and the apadana of Artaxerxes II.

The numerous foundation inscriptions of Darius' palace indicate that it was constructed early in his reign (his grand-father, Hystaspes, was still alive) and that the building was erected on a brick platform in the Babylonian manner. Its plan is that of an Assyrian or Elamite palace, and it has been compared to the palace of Sargon II at Khorsabad in Assyria, the pre-Achaemenid western part of the Southern Fortress of Babylon which adjoins the 'Persian Building', and more significantly to the Elamite palace at Tchoga Zambil. The enor-mous area of the palace (820 × 490 ft) is divided by three inner courts ranged from east to west. Around these, larger and smaller rooms are constructed of mud brick upon baked-brick foundations and the whole was surrounded by a high mud-brick wall. The entrance on the eastern side leads into the first court through a gateway lined with famous glazed-brick panels depicting the Immortals, the picked bodyguard of the king arrayed in embroidered ceremonial dress with a full skirt and sleeves and a twisted turban, each holding his spear at the 'present arms' position. A wide corridor led directly into the first open court (106 × 118 ft), part of which was lined with glazed-brick panels including a representation of a winged

Fig. 24

disc and a pair of confronted human-headed lions wearing Babylonian crowns. On the north side of this court were two identical narrow reception halls and a passage leading north-wards into the apadana building. In the region of this passage were fragments of another set of glazed-brick panels with striding lions very similar to those of the processional way at Babylon, and it is thought that these decorated a wall dividing the apadana from the palace. West of the first open court and separated from it by a suite of three rooms lies a smaller and more enclosed court around which the royal quarters were most probably grouped. Further west lay a large hall with an outside entrance and a raised platform on the southern side. Around this hall were found parts of glazed-brick panels of winged bulls, griffins, and also spearmen. It seems likely that the panels of the western entrance repeated on a less lavish scale the procession of Immortals of the eastern gateway. A few bits of stone sculpture found south of these buildings show that tribute-bearers and animals carved in the same style as those of Persepolis played some part in the later constructions at Susa, but we cannot tell precisely where they belonged. The panels of enamelled bricks, performing the function of tapes-tries, were the chief decorative feature of Darius' palace. The composition of the blue, white, yellow and green glazes is copied from Babylon as are the designs of the bulls, lions and rosette borders, but the antithetically placed sitting sphinxes (or androcephalous lions) are best paralleled at an earlier date in Sargon's palace at Khorsabad. The composite griffins with the forefeet of lions and the hind legs of eagles, goats' horns, ears, etc. are originally Median.

The apadana on the north side of Darius' palace, is the work of Artaxerxes II, in whose reign Susa was the favoured winter residence and the favourite hunting ground for the intrigues of the queen mother, Parysatis. Inscriptions on the column bases assure us that Artaxerxes was merely recon-

Fig. 24. Lion-griffin of multi-coloured glazed bricks, Susa. Total height of panel, 5 ft 3 in. (85)

structing an earlier apadana built by Darius on almost the same spot and later gutted by fire. The apadana as rebuilt by Artaxerxes nearly a century later is an almost precise replica of that at Persepolis with its thirty-six majestic columns of the central hall arranged in a square of six with porticos of two rows of six columns on two sides. The execution of the great bull capitals and side volutes differs but slightly from those of Persepolis, and visitors to the Louvre will have been impressed by the massiveness of the example housed there.

Fig. 25

Persepolis was, as conceived by Darius, not a capital in the political sense, for it was not counted by the Greeks along with the other capitals, Babylon, Susa and Sardis, but a ceremonial shrine largely reserved for the celebration of the Persian New Year festival which had acquired an imperial significance. Darius was responsible for the master plan of the terrace, stairways and official buildings which occupy most of the area of the site; it was completed by Xerxes. Artaxerxes I in turn finished some additions which Xerxes had begun. Excavation has been the work of many hands, but the scientific survey and publication of Persepolis has become available only in recent times by the work of the Oriental Institute of the University of Chicago under the direction of Dr Erich Schmidt.

Fig. 26
Plate 37

All the structures of Persepolis were built on an artificial terrace standing about 40 feet high and measuring 1,500 by 900 feet. The terrace abuts on to mountain scarps on the northern and eastern sides, so that a good deal of levelling was necessary. Side by side across the centre of the terrace were erected the two largest buildings: the apadana or Audience Hall of Darius, and the Throne Hall of Xerxes, also known as the Hundred Column Hall (J and M on the plan). These important build-ings bisect the terrace into two functional areas. On their northern side was the military quarter, parade ground and ceremonial area, whilst the southern part of the terrace was occupied by the palaces of Darius (I), Xerxes (F), the Harem (C) and the large Treasury complex (B). The layout of the southern area was largely completed in the time of Xerxes, though the Unidentified Palace (H) in the south-western corner is a hotchpotch possibly built by Artaxerxes III, and it is probably he who constructed a rock-cut tomb (P) in the hill-side immediately to the east of the terrace. The layout of the northern part of the terrace was the work of Xerxes and Artaxerxes I. The main (only?) access to the terrace was by the great north-western stairway (L) which led to the monumental gate of Xerxes (K). In the time of Artaxerxes II a processional way led from Xerxes' gate to a second gate (N) which in turn gave access to the court in front of the Hundred Column Hall of Xerxes. The passage between the northern and southern areas of the platform, and the west-east passage between the Audience Hall and Palace of Darius and the Hundred Column Hall and Treasury was made through the building (E), often called (after Herzfeld) the Tripylon because of the

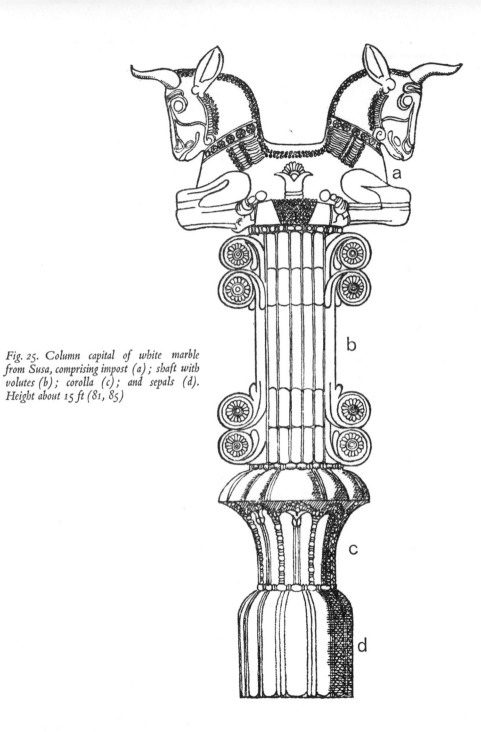

Fig. 25. Column capital of white marble from Susa, comprising impost (a); shaft with volutes (b); corolla (c); and sepals (d). Height about 15 ft (81, 85)

a

b

c

d

Plate 36

three doors leading out of the main room. Schmidt refers to it as the Council Hall, but perhaps the name Central Hall, used here, least begs the question of its function.

Persepolis was founded by Darius shortly after 518 BC. Gold and silver tablets from under the foundations of the Audience Hall (apadana) show that Darius began the building before his Scythian expedition in 513. This was apparently before the final completion of the terrace, since an inscription built into the southern façade refers to 'the lands beyond the sea', i.e. Europe.

The evolution of the Persepolis buildings from Pasargadae and Susa, Darius' earlier capital, was direct. Although at Pasargadae there was no apadana of Susa and Persepolis type, the square and rectangular pillared halls and porticos found at Pasargadae are the basic architectural units of Persepolis, whilst the gateway of Xerxes at Persepolis is a clear copy of the Pasargadae hypostyle gatehouse. The same combination of stone and mud brick, with the doorways and window-like openings constructed of massive stonework and the intervening wall spaces of quickly deteriorating mud brick, is the same at both sites, as are the double animal columns and the wooden stuccoed pillars used throughout the Persepolis Treasury. But amongst the innovations are some of the most attractive features of Persepolis – the double-turn staircases (which have no obvious prototype), bell-shaped column bases, fluted columns, and the Egyptian cavetto mouldings of the door lintels. For all its great sophistication, however, Persepolitan architecture is full of cumbrous features. The regularity of the architectural units would suggest a certain degree of 'prefabrication', but instead there is a laborious attempt to carve complete doorways from a single block or construct them from unequal blocks; column drums are irregular, not standardised like those of contemporary Ionia; steps are unequal and megalithic, and paving units are 'crazy'. All this, of course, has one obvious

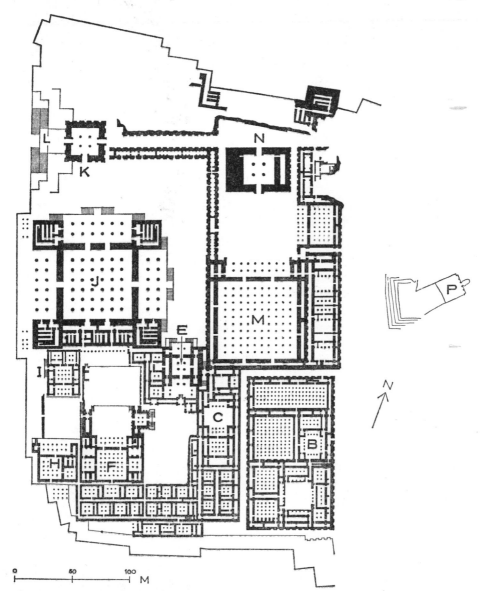

Fig. 26. Plan of Persepolis. B, Treasury; C, Harem; E, Central Hall; F, Palace of Xerxes; H, Unidentified Palace; I, Palace of Darius; J, apadana; K, gate of Xerxes; L, north-western stairway; M, Throne Hall of Xerxes; N, processional gateway; P, rock-cut tomb

explanation: Persepolis is primarily the creation of the sculptor, not of the architect. The aim was not beauty of structure but beauty of treatment: structurally it is retrograde. The standardisation is therefore that of the sculptor and undecorated surfaces remained crude masonry. We should not, of course, make too clear a distinction between mason, architect and sculptor in ancient times to suit our present-day concept, especially as the builders of Persepolis were recruited and trained for a special task. This was the building of a shrine rather than a series of functional buildings, a shrine to embody the importance of the New Year festival.

Thus the decoration of these buildings was unlike anything that went before; it is as if the whole ceremony of the New Year had been photographed and printed on the stone dadoes against which it took place, for the famous sculptures appear loosely to portray the stages of the festival which was the chief reason for the palace's existence. Following the reliefs, we may follow the festival procession in and out of the buildings as finally completed by Artaxerxes I. The delegation from the satrapies assembled on the plain on the west of the terrace and there dismounting from their transports (horses, camels, bulls, horse-drawn chariots and asses), some still wearing travelling cloaks and mufflers, they mounted the terrace by the great north-western stairway and passed through the Gate of Nations built by Xerxes. The whole great pageant was reviewed by the king and the Persian nobility from the western side of the great apadana, for there the projection of the terrace's western side forms a saluting-box commanding the scene. The Persian nobles, as they mounted the apadana by either its northern or eastern stairs, were given a preview in stone of the sight which awaited them on the plain below. On the staircase were carved the figures of the tributaries from twenty-three nations set amongst the young conifers which Darius had planted on the plain. The sculptures on the northern and eastern stairways of

Plate 39

94

the apadana, which the inset inscriptions show were finished by Xerxes, are identical in layout and depict the same event in the same scenes but in the reverse order, so that the figures on the northern staircase face in the opposite direction to those on the eastern staircase. The result is one of the most intriguing achievements of ancient art, for the figures on one staircase show the reverse sides of the figures on the other. This is an entirely new concept which some have attributed to the domin/ating Persian concept of dualism, but for the art historian it not only completes the details of dress and weapons of the reliefs but fully demonstrates the tremendous amount of paper blue/printing of which ancient artists were capable, even though the scheme is incomplete and full of inconsistencies.

The sculptured reliefs of the two sloping stairway parapets show on one side three registers of a procession of tribute/bearers, on the other two registers of Persian and Median nobility moving up to the apadana preceded by a guard of honour of Immortals to survey the assembly. Above the nobles are depicted the royal grooms, stool/bearer and the king's two chariots on their way to take up position for the review. The over/all scheme of decoration is interrupted by the central panel on the front of the middle landing. In the centre of this was an inscription of Xerxes flanked by alternate Median and Persian guards. Over the spot hovers the winged disc of Ahuramazda protecting the king's words. The triangular corners of both the central and side parapets of these stairways are filled by the *symplegma,* the lion attacking the rearing bull. This heraldic device was in some way the symbol of the noble docility of the declining year and the vigour of the new.

After the review there was a banquet, which most probably took place in the Palace of Darius, for on the staircase of this building, apart from the later sculptural additions made by Artaxerxes III, the sculptures mostly portray servitors laden with wine/skins, succulent young animals and dishes of food.

Plate 40

Plates 41, 42

On the jambs of the northern doorways Darius is shown entering the palace accompanied by his towel-bearer and fly-whisk-bearer and holding in his hand a lily. Other doors throughout the building bear representations of attendants carrying towels and scent bottles, and this adds to the suggestion that the Palace of Darius was used as a banquet hall. It is possible that before the banquet a short reception was held in the Central Hall. Here the monumental staircase on the northern side shows the nobility, Medes on one side, Persians on the other, mounting the stairs, each carrying a small lily, the traditional 'hand-out' before an ancient Near Eastern banquet. The atmosphere is informal: the guests turn and chat, sniff their lilies or tap their neighbours on the shoulder. On the south, sculptured servants carry food up the stairs into the building. But in spite of this suggestion that the Central Hall was at one time and in some way connected with the banquet, it appears to have served other purposes and undoubtedly saw the scenes of preparation for the next stage of the ceremony. On the sides of the eastern doorway of the Central Hall Darius is depicted on the *sedia gestatoria* ready for his triumphal entry into the great Throne Hall (M), where everyone was assembled. The throne itself with the crown prince Xerxes standing behind it is set upon a great four-legged dais or divan carried by twenty-eight miniature figures in the varied attire of the tributary nations. Above the dais is a fringed canopy and the protecting figure of Ahuramazda. The same type of portable palanquin is shown on a grander scale in the Throne Hall itself and on the Achaemenid tomb façades at Naqsh-i Rustam. It is likely that the enthroned king and crown prince were actually carried on ceremonial occasions by a team of bearers from the bounds of the empire.

The southern doorways of the Throne Hall were sculptured with reliefs closely corresponding to those just described. This time, however, it is not Darius and his heir but the heirless

Fig. 27. Artaxerxes enthroned; sculpture on the southern doorway of the Throne Hall at Persepolis (86)

Artaxerxes I and his fly-swatter, for it was under Artaxerxes that this hall was completed.

    The delegates of the tribute nations, having mounted on to the terrace by the north-western stairway and passed the gate of Xerxes and the unfinished gate of Artaxerxes, will be assembled before the portico of the Throne Hall to approach the king and present their gifts. In contrast to the banqueting nobles, the atmosphere amongst the tribute-bearers is seen to be tense. But each group is led by a Persian usher into the royal palace, a noble who places his hand reassuringly on that of the leader of each national group in a spirit of dignified cameraderie. To identify the racial groups is not easy. The Medes and Persians themselves are clear and well dif-ferentiated, in that the Medes wear domed hats with attached

Fig. 27

ribbon, belted coat, long trousers and belted shoes; over the shoulders of most of them is draped a long topcoat with empty sleeves. Their typical weapon is a short sword with a decorated scabbard having Scythian features. The Persian nobles wear a fluted tiara, flowing *candys,* a loose garment consisting of skirt and jacket with full sleeves, and belted shoes. Medes and Persian ushers and officials appear to have played equal roles at functions, and the contrast between the light pleated Persian dress and the stiff leather dress of the Medes is a striking one. Both Medes and Persians carry identical bow cases of leather and wear the same types of earrings and torques. Close to the Persians in dress are the Elamite guards from Susa – the Immortals – who are identical with those on the glazed tiles at Susa.

No final identification of the tribute delegations is possible. The lists of the nations in Herodotus (III, 90) agree neither in content nor in order with the inscriptions of Darius, both on his Persian monuments and his Suez stela. The number of satrapies increased from twenty-three to thirty-one between the writing of Darius' Behistun inscription and the *daiva* inscription of Xerxes. Twenty-three nations are in fact depicted on the apadana staircase reliefs, but these do not correspond exactly to the Behistun list. A few nations can of course be safely identified by dress, facial features or attributes, but the final and surest source of information has not yet been fully exploited. This is the detailed study of the figures which uphold the royal thrones on the rock-cut tomb façades of Naqsh-i Rustam. There on Darius' tomb twenty-nine tributary figures correspond to the twenty-nine satrapies listed in the accompanying inscription, whilst figures on the tomb of Artaxerxes II have small cuneiform labels attached. Besides Medes, Persians and Susians, R. D. Barnett has listed as securely identified by a combination of internal and Naqsh-i Rustam evidence, together with ethnographical details taken from Herodotus, the

following nations named by Darius: Armina (Armenians); Plate 39
Haraiva (Arians); Harakhuvatiya (Arachosians); Saka Tigrakhauda (pointed-hat Sakae); Parthava (Parthians); Asagartiya
(Sagartians), all of which have basically Median dress with
differentiating headgear or weapons. Related in dress are the
Bakhtrish (Bactrians) with their Median coats but baggy cotton
trousers. The Babiruviya (Babylonians), the only Mesopotamian
people, are identified by their conical caps with tassels; Arabaya
(Arabians) with dromedary; Putaya (Libyans) with kudu;
Kushiya (Ethiopians) with their negroid features and tribute of
ivory and young giraffe (or okapi?) all clearly discernible, but
identification of Mudraya (Egyptians) is tentative because of
damage to the reliefs. Hindush (Indians) are bare-chested
and bring gold-dust and asses; Skudra (Skudrians) can be
recognised by the Thracian helmets of classical art and their
characteristically light shields mentioned by Herodotus. From
the peoples of Asia Minor only the Katpatuka (Cappadocians)
with Phrygian fibulae fastening their cloaks seem plausibly
identified. A group frequently treated as Syrians wear the boots
more typical of Asia Minor and a cloak with a single corner Plate 38
tassel found on Ionian sculptures, and are identified by Barnett
as Lydians. A similar cloak is worn by a group identified as
Yauna (Ionians). 'Cilicians' now appear to be identifiable as
Sogdians, whilst Choresmians, Drangianians, Gandarians
and other groups are doubtful.

Entering the Throne Hall, the delegates saw carved on the
doorways the scene they were about to witness. Artaxerxes sits
enthroned behind two smoking braziers surrounded by his
officials and receiving in audience a Median noble. Beneath
him the guards are arranged in five registers, representing their
position round the inside walls of the building. The precise
significance of the scene here represented depends on the identity
of the Median noble, a high official carrying his sword of office,
who bows before the king and places his hand to his mouth in

the traditional Persian gesture of subordination. If we take him to be the *Hazarapat,* the chief-of-staff who supervised all external relations, then he is probably introducing to the king the first of the delegations. But because two very similar reliefs showing Darius enthroned and receiving the same Median noble were found in the earliest part of the Treasury buildings, it has been assumed that the Median is the comptroller of the Treasury closing the ceremony by presenting to the king a

Fig. 28

complete account of the assembled tribute. These Treasury reliefs of Darius are of great interest in themselves, for they show the crown prince Xerxes standing behind the royal throne with his head on the same level as that of Darius and with his hand placed on the back of the throne. This conventional way of depicting Xerxes' right of succession was perfectly obvious to all who saw it, and especially to Xerxes. Over the heads of his brothers Darius chose Xerxes as his successor after the battle of Marathon (in 490 B C). These reliefs must therefore date from between this year and Darius' death in 486. Of incidental interest is Herzfeld's suggestion that the messianic title 'Son of Man' used by the prophet Daniel, whose vision shows some acquaintance with the composite beasts of Persepolis-type sculpture, was the official Persian title for the heir to the throne. 'I saw in the night visions, and behold with the clouds of heaven came one like a Son of man and arrived at the Ancient of days, and they brought him near before him. And there was given him dominion and glory and kingship, that all people, tribes and languages should serve him.' These words of Daniel (VII, 13) seem to describe and incorporate the phraseology of the investiture of an Achaemenid prince with the co-regency which both Cambyses and Xerxes enjoyed and which is significantly symbolised in the reliefs in the Treasury buildings.

Various considerations have led the excavators to conclude that the Throne Room or Hundred Column Hall, an un-

Fig. 28. Relief of Darius and his officers from the Persepolis Treasury. Length about 20 ft (86, 92)

necessary extravagance whilst Darius' apadana was still
serviceable, was for the purpose of displaying beside the king
a selection of treasures from the near-by strong rooms of the
Treasury. This 'palace museum' is fully in accordance with the
ceremonial development of the northern part of the terrace in
Xerxes' time. We know nothing from contemporary inscriptions of what the Treasury itself contained, but much of the
tribute pictured in the reliefs is of raw materials, so that we may
imagine that cloth, paper, spices, ivory and skins were stored
there as well as the gold and silver vessels, bullion and gold-
dust. A few exotic objects contained in the Persepolis Treasury
are listed by classical authors: the most unusual are the golden
plane trees and the golden vine with jewelled grapes mentioned
by Athenaeus in his *Gourmets' Club*. The golden vine was
intended as a shade for the king's bed. A relief of Assurbanipal reclining in a vine-shaded bed makes the idea quite
credible.

Material excavated from the Persepolis Treasury contains
but a few poor fragments rejected by Alexander, but parts of
ivory trays and glass, metal and alabaster vessels were found
there. There are no cuneiform records to elucidate the treasure,

and it is rather for the light they shed on fiscal and administrative matters that the clay tablets discovered at Persepolis have great importance.

The excavations at Persepolis have so far brought to light two separate groups of cuneiform tablets. Over a hundred of the Treasury tablets have been published by G. G. Cameron and with few exceptions are records of payments to craftsmen at work on the Persepolis buildings during the last years of Darius' and the first twenty years of Xerxes' reign. They are written in Elamite cuneiform. It is somewhat disappointing that both these archives deal with the domestic affairs of the local Treasury of Parsa and not with foreign tribute or affairs of state; but we at least obtain an insight into the efficient record/keeping methods of the Treasury and into accountancy at the period of the earliest introduction of coinage, when workers and paymasters alike had discovered the convenience of part/payment in cash along with wages paid in sheep and wine. Cash payments appear to have come into use in 493 B C and the value of a shekel of silver seems to have been fixed by royal edict in terms of sheep and wine. The value of silver and current weights and measures were, as still in England, guaranteed by the Crown, and indeed a number of weights with Achaemenid royal inscriptions survive. Although Darius facilitated this rate by the introduction of minted coinage, the system was originally a Babylonian one, and it is interesting to note that the rate of exchange for silver at Persepolis was close to that found in Babylonian transactions dated to the reigns of Cyrus and Cambyses, and proportionately higher than the exchange under Nebuchadnezzar.

The use of Elamite for book/keeping was more likely deter/mined by the nationality of the accountants than by inherent convenience: probably Darius transferred to Persepolis part of the office staff of his Susa palace. The tablets, as Cameron shows, are file/copies kept by the Susian scribes of requests for payment to workmen, probably made in Aramaic on parchment by official overseers. When the payment had been effected, the Treasury clerks made an Elamite record on clay of the request and payment, and tied it with string to the Aramaic original before putting it on the shelf. Fire or decay have removed all traces of parchment and string.

Not all the employees mentioned in the tablets worked at Persepolis: there are herdsmen and vineyard workers in the country, and tax-gatherers. But the majority are the artisans employed building, 'hod-carrying', and 'gold-inlay workmen making reliefs', 'copperers', 'stone sculpture makers at Parsa' – the local name for Persepolis. Carians, Syrians, and Ionians are listed among them. There is evidence to suggest that similar wage records were kept at Susa, where by a gigantic effort at international co-operation artistic elements from many parts of the subject lands were fused into the astonishingly accomplished Achaemenid style of art and architecture. In the course of the excavations at Susa since 1898 the following foundation text laid by Darius on marble and clay tablets in many parts of the building has been assembled. It is known as the Susa Magna Carta. The translation roughly keeps the typically Persian grammatical structure of the original.

The Great God is Ahuramazda, who has created this earth, who has created yonder sky, who has created mankind, who has created welfare for man, who has made Darius king, the one king of many, one lord of many.

I am Darius, Great King, King of kings, king of peoples, king of this earth, son of Hystaspes, an Achaemenian.

And Darius the King says: Ahuramazda, the greatest of the gods, he created me; he made me king; he granted to me the kingdom that is great, with good horses, with good men.

By the grace of Ahuramazda, my father Hystaspes and Arsames my grandfather, they were both living when

Ahuramazda made me king on this earth. It was the wish of Ahuramazda to make me alone king and he made me king on this earth. I worshipped him: Ahuramazda brought me aid. What I commanded to be done, that he made successful. What I did, I did it all by the grace of Ahuramazda.

This palace which I erected at Susa, its materials have been brought from afar. The earth was dug deep until bedrock was reached. When the earth had been thoroughly excavated, the rubble was packed in, one part forty cubits, one part twenty cubits deep. On that rubble the palace was erected. That the earth was thoroughly excavated, and that the rubble was packed in, and that unbaked bricks have been moulded – all this was the work of Babylonians.

And timber, cedar, this was brought from a mountain named Lebanon; the Assyrian folk, it brought it to Babylon and from Babylon Carians and Ionians brought it to Susa. *Yaka*wood [teak?] was brought from Gandara and Carmania. Gold was brought from Sardis and from Bactria and wrought here. And precious stones – lapis lazuli and carnelian [?] which were worked here, these were brought from Sogdiana, and turquoise [?] was brought from Choresmia. And silver and ebony were brought from Egypt. And the material with which the wall of the palace was painted, that was brought from Ionia. And the ivory which was wrought here, that was brought from Ethiopia and from Sind and from Arachosia. And the stone pillars which were fashioned here, these were brought from a palace called Abiradus in Elam.

The masons who wrought the stones, they were Ionians and Sardians. The goldsmiths who wrought the gold, they were Medes and Egyptians. And the men who worked on the wood, they were Sardians and Egyptians. The men who worked on the baked bricks, they were Babylonians. And the men who adorned the wall, they were Medes and Egyptians.

And Darius the King says: At Susa splendid things were ordered and splendid things were achieved. Me may Ahuramazda protect, and Hystaspes who is my father and my people.

There is little doubt therefore about the international co-operation in the building, but the absence here and in the Treasury tablets of a precise reference to the nationality of the sculptors only aggravates the problem of the origin of Achae-menid sculptural style. From Assyria the palace sculptors took over the low relief, linear treatment, detail of hair and beards as well as the conventional portrayal of royal figures in exag-gerated size. The main differences which set Achaemenid sculpture apart from ancient Near Eastern reliefs are, firstly, its abandonment of the didactic themes and 'large canvases' of Mesopotamian work; secondly, the greater plasticity and roundedness of the figures in contrast with the flat raised sur-faces of Assyrian reliefs and the raised drawing of Egyptian work; thirdly, there is the treatment of draperies and the con-cern with the relation of draperies to the underlying contours of the body. Controversy around the second and third of these distinctions centres on the amount of direct Ionian Greek influence. Greek sculptors undoubtedly worked at Persepolis: we have not only information in classical authors but evidence in the form of graffiti on the stonework of Persepolis of Greek heads exactly corresponding to those on red-figure vases. But Frankfort, it seems to me, is wrong in attributing the modelling and plasticity of the Persepolis reliefs to Ionian influence. True, Near Eastern stone reliefs had remained essentially flat, but a higher degree of plasticity and successful three-quarter relief was achieved by the 'Phoenician' ivory workers of North Syria in the eighth century, and in view of the prevalence of Syrians and ivory workers at Persepolis we should not consider the Persepolis reliefs merely *vis-à-vis*

Mesopotamian stone reliefs. Rather we should regard it as a new formula largely influenced by such minor arts as ivory carving. This would also explain the 'restraint' of the Persepolis reliefs which worries those who derive them from the accom-plished vigorous work of Greek Asia Minor; but it does not, of course, help our essential understanding of how the new style was formed and maintained. It is fairly generally accepted that the drapery at Persepolis is rendered in a formula de-veloped in early sixth-century Archaic Greek art. The stacked zigzag folds on the sleeves and on the lower parts of the Persians' robes are treated identically on earlier Ionian sculp-ture, and the artistic contrast in the curly folds and the severe outline of the body beneath the thin robe is the result of Greek aesthetics at Persepolis. There is Urartian evidence for the inlaying of statuary with gold and lapis lazuli as also practised in Achaemenid sculpture. The brilliant polish on the surface of many reliefs was a new feature and indicates that only minor details could have been painted.

It is impossible to recapture the full aesthetic effect: we know nothing of the mud-brick walls which towered above the sculptured stairways and dwarfed them. At Persepolis the indications are that the bricks were plain, but undoubtedly tapestries, copper sheets and other forms of decoration were used. The sculpture of Persepolis is thus intimate eye-level sculpture, catching the eye, but not engaging the mind in contemplation as did the great sculptures of the Assyrian palaces. It served to give the visitor a feeling of stability rather than awe of the powers of sovereigns at war. If we understand this, we can forgive its monotony.

Whilst the Achaemenids to some extent (particularly in the Susa palace) adopted the constructional and decorative techniques of Mesopotamia, their pillared halls and porticos, the raised platforms, monumental staircases, and the shape of the columns themselves appear as a clean break with Near

Eastern tradition. How original were they in these features? Granting the great originality of the synthesis, archaeologists have conjectured the ancestory of various architectural elements, especially of the apadana, tracing it to Babylon, Egypt and the Syro-Hittite architecture of north Syria. In the present climate of discovery in Iran we cannot now dismiss Median architecture as of no account, as many scholars have done. Even though Ecbatana is unexcavated and we do not possess a single building of the Medes, greater availability of Mesopotamian cuneiform records lead us to the conclusion that the Medes were substantial builders. If we ascribe importance to their minor arts, we should be prepared to accept the influence of their architecture and reconsider the suggestions of Marcel Dieulafoy and other early excavators that Achaemenid architecture contains a strong vernacular element of timber construction of the mountain dwellers of north Iran. The rock-cut tomb façades at Naqsh-i Rustam show the dentils of the beam ends and the heavy timber construction of the roofs. The four-pillar porticoes and the low central doorways of the tombs appear to reproduce the frontage of a type of peasant dwelling until recently in use in Mazanderan and the Elburz, and recorded by Dieulafoy and other travellers. In these dwellings, the tombs and the great apadana, we see the same cardinal principle of Persian architecture – to cover a square area with a heavy insulating roof on a forest of regularly placed columns. The area can then be completely enclosed by curtain walls (which take no weight) or only partially enclosed in order to leave porticoes around the sides.

When we in fact turn to the mountainous north, we cannot fail to be impressed by a building uncovered by the Russian excavations at Arin-berd in Soviet Armenia on the populous northern boundary of Urartu. Here is virtually an apadana, a square building of mud brick, brightly painted, with its roof supported by six rows of five regularly placed columns. The dilemma about this building is that the date of its foundation cannot be established. Is it the ancestor of the apadana or was it built as a result of the considerable Achaemenid activity in Armenia? The debris in the upper layer inside the building is late sixth–fifth century, and it is therefore plausible that it was founded before Xerxes, whose building activities in this region are known. A less impressive columned hall can be cited from eighth-century Karmir Blur, and therefore it appears certain that Urartians had columned halls even if it cannot be shown that they originated the apadana. There are more recent reports, however, that an apadana of pre-Achaemenid date has been found at the Urartian site of Altintepe in the Lake Van region.

Both Ghirshman and Barnett have suggested that building platforms derived from Urartu, where the building of ter-raced fortresses was necessitated by the terrain. Three Persian platforms antedate Persepolis, or are at least thought to do so. Two are in eastern Khuzistan: at Masjid-i Sulaiman, 50 km. south-east of Shustar and Bard-i Nishandah, a mile or two from the banks of the Karun. The third is at Pasargadae, the so-called Takht-i Sulaiman north of the palace area. The two former terrace edifices are built of huge rough stones giving a 'cyclopean' appearance. It is not in fact true-fitted cyclopean masonry such as we find practised in Ionia during the seventh century, but rather a matter of building up huge roughly squared boulders as in many of the fortresses around Lake Van. Beautifully drafted masonry is known to have been used in Urartu and also the same orthogonal masonry as at Persepolis, but the use of iron clamps set in lead to fortify masonry at Pasargadae and Persepolis seems to have been adopted from the Assyrians. A square tower has also been found in the Karmir Blur excavations and is perhaps connected with the square fire-towers at these two Achaemenid sites (p. 174), where re-cessed windows greatly resemble those on the bronze model of a

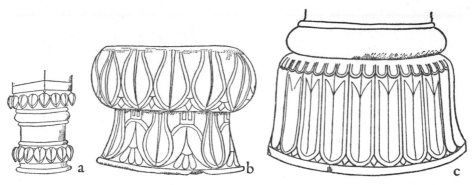

Fig. 29. a, Foliated furniture fitment from Urartu, eighth century B C. Height about 10 in.; b, column capital from Bayrakli (Smyrna), Ionia, early sixth century B C ; c, column base from Susa, sixth century B C, height about 18 in. (79)

Urartian building from Toprakkale in the British Museum.

There is no single source for the distinctive Achaemenid columns; they are composed of multifarious elements, rising from a ring of drooping sepals (d) and a corolla (c), derived from the Egyptian palm-leaf capital. The nearest parallels to the foliated bases come from the Ionian coast, from Neandria, Phocaea and Bayrakli (Old Smyrna), comparable in shape to a base from Susa. According to E. Akurgal these early sixth-century Ionian columns are influenced by Urartu. We know nothing as yet of Urartian columns, but the baluster legs on Urartian furniture with their bosses of downward-curling sepals strongly suggest the origin of the sepal-rings both on Persepolis columns and on the earliest Ionian columns from Neandria, Aegae, Naucratis and Delphi. Cushion-shaped column bases from Syro-Hittite sites in the Turkish Hatay and north Syria (Tell Tainat, Sakjegeuzu, Senchirli) have carved fronds curling over the edges and the double volutes on the cross-legs of a stool on a carving from Senchirli closely parallel the side volutes (b) on Achaemenid columns. We must remember in this connexion that the Aramaean Syro-Hittite kingdoms in

Fig. 25

Fig. 29

Fig. 25

the eighth century had been under the domination of Urartu. The upper and most characteristic part of the column is the impost block shaped into the fore-parts of two animals. This device we have already met in Luristan art, but here again this essentially non-Mesopotamian feature is found in addorsed calves' heads on a Urartian mirror in the British Museum recently published by Barnett and on a white stone dagger pommel from Lake Van in the Louvre. On the mirror, as on the Susa capitals (but not at Persepolis), there is a small lotus between the two *protomai*. Was this device, essentially Iranian, a feature of Median and Urartian art? For the passion of the latter for decorating furniture and vessels with bull and griffin heads is well known.

We are, in short, faced on every side with new evidence suggesting, but not proving, that Urartu and Media were formative influences. We cannot assess the legacy of Elam: Persians surely borrowed Elamite dress and possibly cuneiform, though Persian and Urartian scripts show some similarity. If we claim that the Ionian influence which many have stressed in Achaemenid architecture is not itself *sui generis* but likewise Urartu-inspired, do we not appear a little too Urartu-minded? The complexity of the situation lies mainly in our lack of understanding of the relationship between Urartian and Phoenician art by way of north Syria. The side volutes and sepal rings of Achaemenid columns were elements originally at home in Phoenician art, but I think we must assume that they travelled into Persia by way of Urartu, though no final answer is possible, since the Achaemenid architects were obviously eclectic. The Phoenician-Ionian relationship is further relevant to the Achaemenid problem because of the presence in Kurdistan of rock-cut tombs whose façades are decorated with Ionian-type columns. They are apparently Median work, and there is a particularly fine one at Da-u Dukhtar in Fars itself, sometimes claimed to be the tomb of

Teispes or Cyrus I. Strictly, there is no means of dating it except that the column bases are those of Pasargadae. But the capitals, are they derived from Ionia or do they come to Media, Persia and Ionia from the same source? That source can only have been the 'proto-Aeolic' capitals of Phoenician and Israelite architecture, and a suggestion that it was somehow established in Persia at an early date is to be found on a relief of Sargon II (*c.* 710 BC) from Khorsabad which shows an aedicule not unlike the façade of Da-u Dukhtar and with very similar columns. It stands along with a Persian fire-altar in heavily-wooded hill country, probably Media. Rock-cut tombs, admittedly without façades, are numerous around Karmir Blur, and we may accept the Urartian region as the obvious source for the Achaemenid custom of rock-chamber burial, rather than look beyond to Asia Minor.

Ionians were certainly employed as craftsmen at Susa and Persepolis, but their influence in architecture seems negligible. Although stress has been laid on the widespread use of columns in contemporary Ionia and Persia, the Achaemenid usage of columns is in fact closer to that of Egypt. Darius in the Egyptian temple he built at Khargeh Oasis used columns for a hypostyle hall and, according to Diodorus Siculus, Cambyses had employed builders from Egypt. The lotus corolla element in the columns, the cavetto mouldings over the doors, as well as the massive mouldings of the doorways themselves are all elements the Achaemenids derived from Egypt. Column torus and flutings are, however, most clearly paralleled in Ionia.

In summary, although the problem of Achaemenid archi-tecture has not lost its complexities by recent discoveries, the case for the legacy of a Median architecture with a heavy Urartian component has given a clearer insight into what it borrowed from outside and what it could claim as an indi-genous vernacular style.

CHAPTER VI

Achaemenid Arts

THE INTERNATIONALISM of the Achaemenid empire is reflected not only in laws and chronicles and in the use of Aramaic as an international administrative language but also in the unity of style of works of art in all media. In the decoration of the monumental palaces commanded by the King of Kings, the magnificent reliefs appear to have sprung full-blown from the workshops of craftsmen recruited, so the inscriptions inform us, from all quarters of the empire. Persepolis was a 'Palace of All Nations', and the inscriptions of Darius and Xerxes stress the international co-operation of the workmen who built and decorated it; yet the resulting integrity of the art style is astonishing.

No great works of art can, of course, be entirely reduced to their sources, and so it is with the reliefs of Persepolis and Susa, where the new vision and design transcends the art itself. This vision was based on the Achaemenid concept of empire. Although still in part at least a prolongation of Assyrian art, the use of the column and apadana gave to Achaemenid architecture the possibilities of a new grandeur which itself embodied a dignified purpose. Gone from the reliefs is the note of savagery and war, macabre rows of prisoners and refugees, which had dominated Assyrian art, giving it a brutal self-satisfaction. The Achaemenid themes are contemplative rather than active, and even where a note of conflict has been retained, as in the scenes of the king killing a lion or monster, or the struggle between the lion and the bull, there is now a spiritual transformation: these scenes no longer represent crude conflicts but the opposing forces of dualism, good against evil, light against darkness, order against chaos, empire against barbarity and, in the case of the battling bull and lion, the renewal of the year. For the rest, we have peaceful processions of guards and tribute-bearers carrying gifts. Just as the Achaemenid rulers had the vision to endow their vast empire with a more ordered concept of life, so their art was capable of conveying an extraordinarily vivid impression of the system of ordered movement. It is sometimes criticised for its seeming lack of expression in its portrayal of the human face; but this may well be an expression of the same sense of detachment, which was more interested in the group than in the individual, although prepared in other ways, for example in the detailed treatment of individual costume, to give some token of the individuality of the figures represented. Yet even here the royal sculptors aimed to suppress outlandish details of hair and dress in order to give a common denominator of cultural unity to the tribute-bearers from all corners of the empire: no stress was laid on anthropological diversity.

This tendency is particularly apparent in the tribute-bearers' gifts. Whilst some offer the raw products of their homeland, horses from Cicilia, balls of cotton from Hindush, others bring objects of Achaemenid metalwork in a style which seems to have been widespread through the satrapies and makes them the most important surviving pieces representing the Achaemenid crafts. It is not known whether there were workshops producing works of this kind in the Achaemenid style throughout the empire, but two factors most probably led to the spread of Achaemenid taste: firstly the predisposition of Persian officials to travel with elaborate appointments and mess-kits, most probably taking Persian-trained craftsmen with them; secondly, the international recruitment of craftsmen for work on Persepolis, which acted as a focus. Craftsmen would return to their home countries with a thorough knowledge of the international style.

The art of the sculptor was followed closely by that of the seal-engraver, and the considerable number of Achaemenid

Fig. 49

cylinder seals is a clear indication that the unity of the style was not the achievement of the sculptors alone. Many Achaemenid seals copy Assyrian themes; the king is shown hunting lions from a chariot or hunting on foot with bow and arrow, both favourite themes of Mesopotamian royal iconography. But the royal hunt is now endowed with religious and cosmic meaning; the king hunts down evil or chases the beasts of the constellations in order to maintain the seasonal rhythm. Wild boars are frequently hunted by the king, and the boar hunt remained a favourite theme of the royal artist in Sassanian times. A number of cylinders depict the circlet of Ahuram-azda placed between heraldic animals or else as a great winged disc supported by two bull-demons after the ancient Hurrian manner. Occasionally the cylinders appear to refer to historical events; there are battles between Persian and Thracian foot-soldiers, and processions of Phoenician or Egyptian captives, but few seals can be dated closely. Some thirty-six are dated by their inscriptions in terms of royal years and extend from the thirty-second year of Darius I to the sixteenth year of Artaxerxes III. Some of these seals have trilingual cuneiform inscriptions, but numerous seals used by merchants and officials bear Aramaic or Phoenician script.

Fig. 50

A second class of seals, in the shape of circular stamps, pose an artistic problem. Whilst many of them bear much the same designs as the cylinders, though without the royal themes, many are cut with single figures in a style which has been claimed as Greek. It is still uncertain whether seals of this class are the work of Greek gem-cutters resident in Persia or that of advanced Persian artists from whom the Greeks learned these techniques. On the whole, however, since it is the dress and facial features of the figures on these seals that are Greek whilst the figures are in most cases oriental, the possibility that they are the products of a school of gem-cutters in Asia Minor cannot be ruled out.

In seals and other products of the minor arts, what Achaemenid art lacked in originality and invention it made up in technical excellence. Recent years have brought to the antiquities market an impressive number of new finds, excellent in preservation and astonishing in their perfection: gadrooned metal cups and vases, amphorae with spouted handles, rhyta or drinking horns, metal fittings for furniture, costume jewellery, carved stone bowls, lapislazuli sculptures, glassware and textiles. Besides those from Persia herself, new pieces come from Greece, Turkey, Babylonia, Siberia, the Caucasus and Altai, supplementing pieces known from Egypt, Palestine, Syria and Pakistan; most are tablepieces of gold and silver toreutic, an art in which the Achaemenids excelled.

The lavishness of the Persian dinnerservices made a deep impression on the Greeks, especially on the frugal Spartans, whose general, Pausanias, after the battle of Plataea ordered a banquet to be prepared in both the manner of Sparta and Persia, using the royal tent and captured equipment of the Persian generals. Such was the dazzling magnificence of the profusion of cups, couches and exotic foods of the Persian table that Pausanias, calling together his fellow generals, exclaimed, 'Men of Hellas, I called you here because I desire to show you the foolishness of the leader of the Medes, who, with such provision for life as you see, came hither to take away from us ours that is so humble.' These were the vessels from which, in the Persian homeland, the famous wine of Shiraz was drunk. On some of the Persepolis tablets vintners and winepresses are mentioned, and the evidence suggests that Shirazi wine was famous even then, whilst Strabo records that the *halubion* wine from the Pontic grapes grown at Halwan in Syria was drunk by the kings of Susa. There sprang up therefore a happy relationship between the oenophilist and the metalsmith.

In the Treasury tablets and palace inscriptions it is the Egyptians who are mostly employed along with Medes as goldsmiths and silversmiths. Silver was in fact brought from Egypt, gold from Bactria and Sardis, to be worked at Susa. Sardis was in control of the Greek gold mines at Thasos and Pactolis, Bactria in control of the newly-tapped sources of gold in Siberia, already exploited by the Scythians. Egyptian influence in Achaemenid toreutics can be traced in a number of specific ways, but so far no precise and direct antecedent of the Achaemenid shallow drinking bowl with its petal-like fluttings and ovoid bosses has been found in Egypt. The idea of the silver wine service was originally Egyptian, and examples of shallow drinking bowls shaped like lotus-blooms are common in Egypt of the XVIII Dynasty; but shallow bronze bowls with radial fluting are found at Early Dynastic Susa and are known in the Luristan repertoire. Although faience bowls with radial lotus stems are known from XXV Dynasty times, the developments which led to the exaggeration of the spaces between the petals to form ovoid bosses seems to have taken place outside Egypt. Possibly the Egyptian silversmiths working in Persia fused the Egyptian lotus bowl with the fluted Iranian bowl. Closely allied in technique to the bowls are thistle-shaped flasks with lotus petals covering the body. The shape is found in silver vessels of the XXV Dynasty and in a treasure of XIX Dynasty silverware from Tell Basta in Egypt, consisting of thistle-shaped flasks and wine jugs with handles in the form of leaping goats, and having globular fluted bodies. It is from these handles that the Achaemenids copied their animal-shaped vessel handles, but at present there is a considerable chronological gap between the Persian vessels and their Egyptian prototypes. Whilst therefore a high degree of dependence on Egyptian styles is likely, we cannot at present point to specific examples of sixth-century Egyptian toreutic which might have been transmitted to Persia. Both the thistle-shaped flask and the shallow wine bowl are found amongst the Assyrian pottery of Sargon's day and were doubtless current in metal work in Mesopotamia before the time of the Achaemenids.

The common problem facing all discussion of Achaemenid metallurgy is that of animal style: unlike sculpture, the minor arts of metalwork appear to have continued over a long period, to merge eventually into the styles of the Classical world; scarcely any pieces come from a dated context. Since now, however, we have rich pre-Achaemenid works from Ziwiyeh and remarkably preserved pieces from Hamadan, we are in a position to see a greater evolution and continuity of style and can appreciate more clearly than the writers of Pope's *A Survey of Persian Art* in 1938 the close links between the minor arts of Assyria and those of Achaemenid Persia. It now seems not unreasonable to assume that the closer the style of any piece to those of Ziwiyeh, the earlier it is likely to be and also that the Hamadan finds, in that they come from the old Median capital, reflect the archaic Median forerunner of Achaemenid art. At the other end of the time-scale is the merging of the Achaemenid animal style into that of Ionian and Crimean Greek ornaments of the fourth century B C and later still, in the third century, a transition from Achaemenid to south Russian Scytho-Sarmatian styles. Thus there appears a helpful polarity which has some likely but uncertain chronological value.

It can now be seen that the representations of animals both in stone and metal derive the stylised hair patterns, formally delineated muscles and arched necks from the crouching bulls and lions on the backs of which the Urartian gods are shown standing, such as the four bronze statues which Barnett has shown were once part of the great throne from Toprakkale in Van. A bronze lion from Anzavur in Van published by Y. Boysal is the direct ancestor, even in its proportions, of the lion rhyta in the Teheran and Metropolitan Museums (see below). There is the same folded ear, puckered nose and ruff encircling the face; even the stylised 'bell-flower' delineation

Fig. 32

on the outstretched forelegs. The relationship of the griffin of the Beyeler rhyton to Urartian and Ziwiyeh griffins is obvious and, in general, the Achaemenid preference for crouching animals and monsters of composite form appears to follow Urartian rather than Assyrian tastes. The griffin and horned-lion monster were peculiar to Urartu, and although Urartian animals are generally wingless, winged lions are represented on some engraved bronze plaques from Altintepe in Van. The transmission of this animal style through Median art is something we cannot yet follow in detail, but the radiation of Urartian influence into Mannaean and Median territory is very apparent in the Ziwiyeh treasure. It is most certainly to the Medes, following a Luristan idea, that Achaemenid art owes the characteristic addorsement of the Urartian-derived beasts, since the motif can be traced back to early seals at Susa. In fact, however, the double animal *protomai* are not at all common in the minor arts.

Three drinking cups with double handles in animal form and friezes of animals thus appear to belong to the very begin-ing of Achaemenid toreutics: indeed they are probably Median vessels and, as the only extant examples of the treasures which made Ecbatana famous before ever Pasargadae or Persepolis were built, we should look at them in detail. Probably the earliest is a two-handled gold cup in the Kevorkian Collection, reported to come from Luristan. The handles are in the form of slender lions whose bodies are scooped to take inlays of paste and precious stones. On the body of the vessel there is a panel of two pairs of lions in profile, but each pair shares the same frontally-facing head in high boss. Whilst this idea is totally inartistic, there is no doubt that it and the general work-manship of this cup are descended from the art of Ziwiyeh and the Amlash beakers, whilst the idea of the twin lions sharing a common head is found at Ziwiyeh, on dress-plaques from Hamadan and on certain Luristan bronzes. The pattern

Plate 26

of raised bars on the rumps of the lions is similar to the raised ribs of the double-headed mountain goats which form the handles of the unique two-handled cup in the Cincinnati Art Museum. This also has a frieze of lions but they are winged and are closer to the Ziwiyeh lions than those of the Kevorkian cup. The drawing of the lions and the border of fan-palmettes on the Cincinnati cup is very close to those of the plaques from Ziwiyeh and a gold Median strip in the British Museum. Unlike the Kevorkian cup, the body of which is covered with simple horizontal ribs, the Cincinnati cup has harsh gadrooning of eggs-and-tongues, more pronounced than any gadrooned piece in Egypt, but similar to the later work of the gold drinking cups from Hamadan. The double-headed-goat handles are unique.

Plate 27

Plate 24

Plates 44, 45

The third two-handled vessel, of silver, whilst probably also Median work, is considerably muted in design and in this more closely approaches what we know to be the Achaemenid style proper. The two rearing bulls which form the handles have, however, distinctively Urartian features and are certainly much earlier than any comparable Achaemenid animals. It seems probable that these three Median vessels are to be placed chronologically in the order in which they have been described here, and show a rough progression from a harsh style and unbalanced composition to something softer and better integrated. When examples of what we might call Median art are so few in number such a general argument is of course open to question. If the comparison with Ziwiyeh art holds good, then we might feasibly place all these vessels between 620 and 550 BC.

Plate 28

None of the gadrooned drinking bowls can be shown to be so early, but since shallow bowls were used for drinking wine by both the Assyrians and Urartians, it is likely that they were used from the earliest times by the Medes. A considerable number of Achaemenid drinking bowls survive: it is difficult

Plates 44, 45

to place them in chronological sequence, but in general the earlier ones are deep and gadrooned over almost the entire surface with raised 'petals' and ovoid bosses. Two gold vessels of this type from Hamadan are inscribed with the name of Darius and are thus the earliest pieces of dated Achaemenid metalware. Later the drinking bowls became shallow and developed a wide, flat rim and appear more suitable for use as plates or 'paterae'. Vessels of this shape appear to have begun in the reign of Xerxes and a number can be attributed by inscriptions to the reign of Artaxerxes I. In their decoration there was a movement away from the schematic gadrooning of

Plate 50
Fig. 43

the lotus-shape and a movement back to the original lotus design of petals, sepals and stamens as well as the use of the lotus-and-bud chain, a design long known in Iran, popular in Assyria and later adopted as the acanthus frieze of Classical art. Probably the finest of all the serving dishes of this later

Plate 54

type is the one from Sinope on the Black Sea. On this the lines of the arc-shaped stems of the lotus-and-bud design have been developed into a cobweb covering the entire surface and the palmettes have been skilfully gilded. A series of paterae with flat central medallions decorated with formal ibex and bull arrangements has recently come to light in Hamadan. Their date is probably late sixth century. The central medallion of one example is filled with the figure of a flying eagle, which is particularly noteworthy since bird designs are rare in Achae-

Plate 53

menid art but popular amongst the Scythians.

But the favourite form of drinking vessel was the rhyton, derived in shape from the barbarian drinking horn. From the

Fig. 30

late second millennium BC pottery drinking horns with basal stands in the form of kneeling animals survive in northern Iran and east Turkey, and the Achaemenid metal rhyta are certainly copies of these. But the same metal-workers' tradition that was responsible for these vessels also produced conical beakers or cups of metal terminating in a perpendicular animal head.

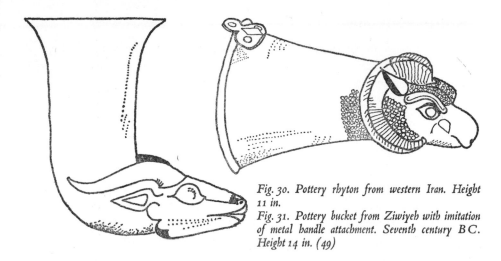

Fig. 30. Pottery rhyton from western Iran. Height 11 in.
Fig. 31. Pottery bucket from Ziwiyeh with imitation of metal handle attachment. Seventh century BC. Height 14 in. (49)

These vessels cannot stand on their own accord and must be held in the hand until drained of their contents. Although these animal-headed beakers are not earlier than the curved horn-rhyta of pottery from Iranian sites, they appear to be earlier than the surviving curved rhyta of metal; but in any case the toreutic traditions of the two types of vessel are closely related, as are a number of whetstone handles from Hamadan and a shield boss (?) from Khafantlu.

Plates 30, 31

Animal-headed beakers and cups were used by the Assyrians in Sargon's day and are depicted in use in the reliefs of his palace at Khorsabad. Some of them were formed into buckets or situlae by having a hoop-handle fixed to the rim with small trefoil attachments. It is possible that they were made by Urartians and were popular amongst the Medes. Animal-headed buckets are carried by Median tribute-bearers engraved on the rim of the Ziwiyeh sarcophagus, and a lion-headed bucket found in a tomb at Gordium in Phrygia probably came there by way of Urartian trade. No ram's-headed examples are known from Assyria, but Ziwiyeh has yielded pottery buckets with rams' heads, retaining the riveted handle attachments of their metal prototypes. Examples of

Fig. 15

Fig. 31

Plate 29

bronze cups from north-west Persia appear to have distinctively Urartian elements in their decoration, and one of these (with an oryx head) is very similar to a cup found in the Lebanon and datable by its cuneiform inscription to about 800 B C. These and other examples seem more archaic than the pottery examples from Ziwiyeh, which in turn have a close relation-ship with two silver examples of ram's-head cups from near-by Khafantlu. These ram's-head cups of pottery and silver, by their progressive degree of stylisation, bridge the period

Plate 49

620–550 B C, when Median art was evolving towards the stereotyped patterns of Achaemenid expression. Indeed, whilst the animal-headed beaker was popular with the Achaemenids and was copied by the Greek potters after they had seen the spoils captured from Mardonius at the battle of Plataea, few actual Achaemenid beakers are known.

Curved rhyta with crouched-animal bases were more popular. Two examples appear to be heavier in composition

Fig. 32

and more Urartian in feature than others, and are therefore possibly earlier. One is in the Galerie Beyeler Collection and has the *protome* of a ferocious griffin as a base; the other is in the British Museum and comes from Marash. It is in the form of a

Plate 32

golden kneeling ram backed by a severe and undecorated silver horn. The brush-like arrangement of hair on the forehead and chest shows overtones of Urartian styling. Two magnificent lion rhyta come from recent finds in Hamadan now in the Teheran and Metropolitan Museums. These have the fore-parts of crouched lions in ferocious posture, the hair of their manes and under-bellies rendered in tiny pointed scales. The lion of the Metropolitan rhyton is closer to lions found in the Ziwiyeh treasure (above all to the lion terminals on the open gold bracelet) especially in its bristling mane and crest, heavily puckered nose and warts between the eyes. Lion heads from tombs at Kelermes in south Russia, dated to about 600 B C, have these same characteristics and therefore it is likely that this

Fig. 32. Gold rhyton, Galerie Beyeler Collection, Basle. Early sixth century B C. Height 6¾ in.

rhyton is of similar date. In all three of these rhyta the horn is of small proportions. The lion of the Teheran rhyton is a tamer beast and closer to lions on the palace sculptures. The rounded wings are like those of animals at Persepolis and Susa, and it is unlikely that these wings were in use before Darius' day. In proportion to the lion *protome*, the horn is large and curved, and this seems characteristic of later rhyta.

Plate 33

Plate 56

The rhyton and animal-headed cup were to survive in Persia well into Sassanian times, when rhyta of large proportions with the heads of bridled horses were especially popular. Amongst the Sassanians, however, the rhyton design followed new drinking habits. In Achaemenid examples the liquid was drunk from the rim as from a normal cup, but in Sassanian rhyta a spout in the animal finial casts out a jet of liquid to be caught in the open mouth as from a Spanish *porro*. There are Achaemenid vessels with triple spouts on the base which must have been for a similar purpose, though no such rhyta are known. It is difficult enough for one person to drink in this manner, but three drinking simultaneously from the same vessel must have been a boisterous party game. Numerous animal-shaped handles originally belonging to similar vessels provide an indication of the progress of animal design towards an organic treatment and naturalistic style. It must be stressed that there are few significant chronological indications to determine this progression. At the opposite end of the scale from the heraldic animals on the cups just discussed are the two silver

Plate 71

handles in the Berlin and Louvre Museums in the form of winged goats. These appear light and sprightly with an expression and perky turn of head copied from nature, but it is significant that, despite the formal rendering of the hair and the gilded hairy tufts on the back haunches, the buttocks are naturalistically moulded and the body is not merely a metal column with a formal surface treatment but is a sensitive and accurate reproduction of the living animal body. The wings, whilst formal, are those of a bird and no longer the curled battens of stiff feathers characteristic of Persepolis art. The lower handle-attachment is purely Greek, and this suggests that classical influences lie behind these superb pieces, which are

Plate 73

usually attributed to the first half of the fourth century B C.

Between these two extremes of style lie numerous handles, chiefly of goat or ibex form. In place of the crude rib-work of earlier examples we find an emphasis on the formal delineation of rump and shoulders in two circular patterns or balancing lobes in order to bring a certain symmetry to the body. This treatment quickly takes shape in a set pattern: a circle is drawn on the rump and shoulders of the animals, representing the cushions of musculature covering the joints of the legs with collar and pelvis. Around this circle are placed two arc-,

Fig. 3

comma- or drop-shaped muscles facing inwards. This circle-and-drop was seemingly a stock treatment in the fifth century and probably survived no later than the early fourth.

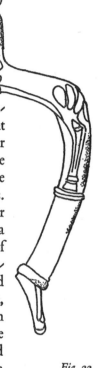

Fig. 33. Pottery rhyton with base spouts.
Azerbaijan Museum. U.S.S.R.

Fig. 34. Silver handle, Brooklyn Museum.
Fifth century B C. Height about 6½ in.

Not all these, of course, are the products of central work‑
shops in Persia. There is at least an indication that an important
toreutic workshop existed in north‑east Asia Minor. Later
examples of handle‑spouted amphorae, which are of course
closely related to the animal‑handled cups, have delicate
flutings on the body, a feature exactly shown on the reliefs.
They appear twice at Persepolis, carried by a tribute‑bearer
who has been identified as a Syrian or a Lydian, and again by a
figure who wears the three‑pointed hat, trousers and sandals of
an Armenian. We should not read too much into these con‑
nections; but the discovery of the archaic example in Syria and
of a superb silver, parcel‑gilt, base‑spouted amphora at Sinope,
which has ibex handles closely related to the Louvre‑Berlin
pair, themselves found in Armenia, all suggest that they were
perhaps Armenian in origin. There is a pottery base‑spouted
amphora from Russian Armenia in the Russian Azerbaijan
Museum.

Fig. 33

Recently it has been discovered that these luxurious items of
table‑ware were imitated in glass. Hitherto Achaemenid glass
has been rare, but the Persepolis excavations yielded a few
fragments of moulded glass bowls with fluted sides, closely
following the shapes of metal bowls. A recently‑discovered
complete moulded‑glass bowl from the Phrygian cemetery at
Gordium in east‑central Turkey is the earliest of a series of such
vessels (about 720 B C), and their manufacture might thus have
begun in pre‑Achaemenid times either in Urartu or Ecbatana.

Plates 58, 59

Plate 46

Fig. 35

Plates 34, 69, 70

Other vessels of white translucent glass closely linked with the later range of metal drinking bowls and antedating the building of the Diana temple in 356 were found at Ephesus. These and the remains of a magnificent rhyton recently unearthed at Persepolis show the close relationship between the glass-moulder and the metalsmith. This rhyton is of solid green glass with traces of lapis lazuli inlay. The base is shaped in the form of a lion attacking a kneeling bull. Naturally glass does not have the survival value of metal, hence the few specimens we possess: on the other hand it was certainly a luxury and does not even appear to have been used for bead-making. Rock crystal was also used: a passage in the *Acharnians* of Aristophanes relates how the Athenian ambassadors were proffered drinks by the Persians in cups of crystal and gold. A bowl of cut crystal in the Cincinnati Museum, whilst it appears to be late Assyrian in manufacture, must have been the prototype for the Persian vessels.

Besides being made into vessels, gold and silver were lavishly used for jewellery. Openwork roundels appear to have been sewn on garments to make an all-over pattern following a Babylonian idea. The cut-out designs in these roundels consist mostly of snarling lions rearing to the inner circumference, their bodies crossed and tails intertwined. Others are filled with horned and winged lions. All the openwork roundels known come from Hamadan, and one or two of them with confronted lions sharing the same head, as on the Kevorkian cup, point to Median work. An important roundel in the collection of the Oriental Institute, Chicago, is a simple circlet containing in its upper part the profile figure of Ahuramazda, a robed and crowned figure in a crescent moon. The lions and griffins of these pieces have fan-shaped manes and are of exactly the same pattern as cut-out animal heads designed for use as pendants on necklaces. Such animal heads were popular with the Scythians and have been found amongst the Greek settlements

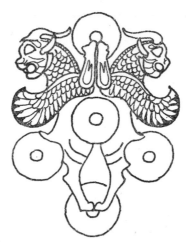

Fig. 35. Gold ornament with a pair of griffins. Metropolitan Museum, New York. Sixth century B C. Height 3⅜ in. (121)

in the Crimea. Gold discs with embossed animal ornament are commonly found in Scythian graves, but in the Achaemenid sphere occur only in the Oxus treasure and at Sardis.

Necklaces and earrings of Achaemenid design are rare. There is a magnificent necklace with openwork pendants of a type just described from Hamadan and a large string of metal pendants and glass beads from a famous tomb in Susa whose contents are now in the Louvre. This tomb is well known for a number of reasons: it was the first recognisably Achaemenid burial that came to light; its contents are outstandingly beauti-ful, comprising besides the necklaces animal-headed bracelets and a pair of penannular earrings inlaid with enamel in blue, white and red. The penannular or fan-shaped earrings of this tomb group have the form that characterises most Achaemenid earrings. The shape appears in the B graves at Siyalk but, apart from an isolated eighth-century example from near Antioch, does not occur again until Achaemenid times when we find it not only in Iran but in the Nebuchadnezzar-Cyrus levels at Ur, Deve Hüyük and Neirab in north Syria, Sardis and other sites where Achaemenid burials or influence are found. It had an influence on the jewellery of the Mediter-ranean world and the Phoenicians spread the type to their

Plate 34

Plate 67

Fig. 44

Plates 68, 42

colonies in Africa, Spain and Portugal. Most examples have an outer fringe of stemmed knobs, and this is particularly evident in the fine example from Egypt in the Louvre. Another type of Achaemenid earring with miniature addorsed animal *protomai* hanging on a slender gold loop is rare and the pair of earrings with miniature parade horses found at Achalgori (cf. next chapter) is unique.

Armlets and necklets appear to have been worn freely by men and women alike, and animal-headed armlets are worn by nobles in the Persepolis reliefs. The wearing of the torque appears to have been introduced into Iran by the Iranian invasion of about 1000 BC, and there are numerous specimens in bronze from Luristan. Although the animal-headed armlet was fashionable in Assyria in the early first millennium, torques were not worn by Assyrians; after Achaemenid times the elaborate torque became a characteristic of Parthian and Sassanian dress and from Parthian sources spread into India as a characteristic of Kushan dress.

Examples from the Ziwiyeh treasure and Hamadan now provide direct links between the penannular armlets of the Assyrians and those typically Achaemenid. Armlets with opposed animal terminals holding between them a disc engraved with a rosette are common on the Assyrian palace sculptures and there are Achaemenid examples in precisely this form. As with vase-handles, there is the same problem of dating the animal style. The lion terminals of a pair of armlets in the grave at Susa, dated by the presence of an Attic coin to the last quarter of the fourth century, have box-like muzzles and pronounced jowls, and these features are characteristic of the terminal of a jug handle in the Oxus treasure from near Samarkand, and of the lions in Sarmatian torques. In the second half of the fourth century the old Median snarling lion had given place to a gentler creature more like a domestic cat. A pair of silver armlets from Vouni in Cyprus terminating

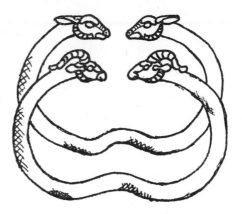

Fig. 36. A pair of gold bracelets from Vouni, Cyprus, dated c. 380 BC. Nicosia Museum. Diameter 2⅞ in. (123)

in rams' heads can be dated by their archaeological context to about 380 BC. In these, as in many, the hoop is constricted by being hammered inwards opposite the aperture.

Fig. 36

To the Sarmatian goldsmiths in particular and to the peoples of barbarian and Celtic Europe in general the Achaemenids transmitted the art of inlaid enamelwork. Whilst inlaid pieces are few, there is little in the ancient world to rival the accomplished style of the two armlets from the Oxus treasure (now in the British Museum and Victoria and Albert Museum), which terminate in the full bodies of winged and horned griffins. They are usually regarded as work of the late fifth century BC, and the arrangement of the cut-away panels on the bodies provides a direct pattern for the earliest Sarmatian inlays on the wings and necks where the inlay was set in tiny cloisons of foil. A very simple forerunner to this inlaid work is now provided by the Kevorkian cup, and we must not overlook a curious bar amongst material from the Kelermes kurgan which has lion-head terminals and cloisons inlaid with amber.

Fig. 42

We are well informed of the weapons of the Achaemenids by the details shown on the sculptures. But in spite of the great arsenals which must have existed to equip the vast armies, very few ordinary weapons have survived. Besides bronze, brass and also probably steel (suggested by linguistic evidence) were used by the Achaemenid armourers. Among the finest examples of Achaemenid goldsmiths' work are two gold daggers from Hamadan. It might be thought that gold was an unsatisfactorily soft metal for weapons, but the booty list of Sargon II after the sack of the city of Musasir in Urartu listed no less than six gold daggers, and Xenophon relates how Cyrus the younger, shortly before he was slain at Cunaxa trying to take the throne from his brother Artaxerxes II, presented a golden dagger to Syenessis, King of Tarsus. The two daggers are reinforced by thick midribs, and both alike have hilts terminating in addorsed lions' heads and quillons in one case formed of lions' claws and in another shaped like ibex heads.

Plate 35

The lion heads on the hilts are typical of Hamadan gold work and derive directly from those on certain plaques in the Ziwiyeh treasure, the muscles on muzzle and cheeks stylised in rounded folds, the nose puckered, the mane rendered in small curled tufts, the hair bordering the face standing up as an encircling ruff, and the ear folded over against the head. Bracelet terminals and lions on the rhyta from Hamadan have precisely these characteristics.

The Ionians and Egyptians are mentioned in the building inscriptions as the ivory workers. Only a few poor specimens of Achaemenid ivory have survived, but it seems that there was a fashion for carved square plaques with representations of animals browsing at a sacred tree: specimens have come from Tell Deim, Persepolis and Susa, at which latter site they show marked Egyptian influence. For the rest, the influence on Achaemenid ivory work is Medo-Scythian and is seen in

Fig. 37

some fifteen surviving examples of trefoil chapes intended for the scabbards of the *akinakes* or Persian short sword. They correspond closely to those carved on the short swords hanging from the belts of Scythians and Medes in the Persepolis reliefs and are roughly trilobate. They are carved with a pattern originally based on the lion-and-bull or lion-and-goat combat.

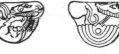

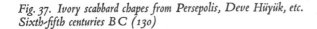

Fig. 37. Ivory scabbard chapes from Persepolis, Deve Hüyük, etc. Sixth-fifth centuries BC (130)

This favourite Persian theme was rolled up in the Scythian manner and the lines of the animal forms reduced to a balance of sinuous elements with concentric lines of folded flesh. Somewhere in its evolution – or debasement – the motif became confused with the Scythian-style single animal enrolled, as found at Pasyryk and in the Scythian tumulus of Seven Brothers. The final product with its detached panels and inserted lotuses was no longer understood by the ivory carvers, and the vitality of the Scythian *animal enroulé* is completely lost.

The Achaemenids appear to have had little interest in sculpture in the round, and most existing pieces must certainly be regarded as belonging to the minor arts. They include a small group of sculptures in soft stones, diorite, lapis lazuli, and blue frit. The largest and possibly the earliest is the royal head in lapis lazuli from Hamadan. Lapis workers are listed in Darius' inscription, and the age-old mines at Badakshan in Afghanistan must still have been active. Two other lapis lazuli sculptures are in the Persepolis court style: one is a figure of a Median noble grasping to his breast a young lion (Cleveland Museum) and another is the human head of a winged bull.

Plates 74, 75

Small free-standing human figures in gold, silver and bronze, about six inches high, are amongst the most appealing of Achaemenid productions and show Medians in ceremonial dress. These are cast but bear the heavy marks of a considerable amount of re-tooling. Two such figures stand in the small model cart of the Oxus treasure. Something of a puzzle is set by a number of bronze ibex heads, all without provenance, and obviously fittings for canopies, chariots or thrones. A head in the Metropolitan Museum has been technically examined and has been found to be made up of five pieces separately cast by the *cire-perdue* process and fused together: but others were

Plate 66

Fig. 41

Plate 65

cast in a single piece. Inside one of the heads is inserted an iron bar, obviously for attachment to a stone or wooden plug. Three joined ibexes, of the exact style of the bronze *protomai*, form the supports of a deep stone bowl, whose shape and fine polish are translated from metalwork. The large size of this vessel and its excellent state of preservation make it all the more tantalising that its place of origin is not known. It is a perfect example of that love of orderliness and tidiness that characterises all Achaemenid art: the juncture of the ibex bodies beneath the base forms a perfectly hexagonal three-pointed star. The interest of this piece is, however, overshadowed by the stone ibex-shaped bowl in the Guennol collection, which is one of the greatest masterpieces of Achaemenid carving.

Plate 61

Plate 60

The close relationship between the sculptor and the bronze-caster demonstrated by these pieces lead us to reflect on the Achaemenid lack of interest in the inherent beauty and qualities of materials. It is not, as some have suggested, that the sculptors' art was derived from that of the metalsmith. How could it be, since carved soft stone or clay or wax models would have been necessary for the casting of the metal statues? It is rather that all materials are treated in the same way as in bronze-engraving, and that the early evolution and perfection of metal arts in Media had a repressive influence on Achaemenid artistic development.

Across this large and varied repertory of minor arts lies the same unifying stamp of Achaemenid uniformity and balance: man, animals, lotus blooms – all are reduced to a pattern as though nature herself were thereby made more comprehensible and tractable. Naturalism is totally out of place, and even that interest in animal life and foliage retained by the Assyrian relief artists has been abandoned. To the vivid battle and hunt-ing scenes of Assyrian art the Achaemenids preferred the static and processional, the symbolic and heraldic, and the circle being the most perfect and economical of all shapes, the aim is most often a circular composition without field or background. Achaemenid art was the art of the isolated object, an art of virtuosity, which, failing fresh sources and inspirations, was bound to end in dull monotony.

It is difficult to imagine how this unformity was achieved and to know how the factors of a common aesthetic were fostered or to determine how far this aesthetic vision was a deliberate part of the cultus of empire. What is apparent, however, from recent discoveries is that Achaemenid taste probably inherited an inborn tendency to symmetry and heraldry from the art of the Medes. Even in the Ziwiyeh treasure the contrast between the active scenes of the Assyrian ivories and the static processional themes of the 'Median' pieces is striking. It seems that the further Achaemenid art became removed from its Median origin, the more its aesthetic sensibilities were con centrated on perfection of craftsmanship, until that 'disparity in harmony' which is the essential of all true art ceased to exist.

It would be remiss in closing this chapter not to mention the impact of Achaemenid art, or that of earlier times, on the Classical world. The direct influence of Iran on the Aegean world begins only in the Orientalising period (*c.* 650–600 BC). Whereas this period of pottery painting in Cyprus, Crete and mainland Greece seems inspired by Syro-Phoenician art, that of Rhodes, with its rows of geese, grazing stags and numerous filling ornaments seems inspired by Luristan ideas: even the painted rays round the bases of the vases, a fashion universal in Corinthian pottery, is found earliest in Persian vase-painting, not elsewhere. The nature of the designs suggests that textiles carried these motifs west, and possibly an independent trade liaison linked Rhodes with south Iran and Elam – inde pendent, that is, of a certain amount of Iranian influence which travelled along the established routes of Greco-Urartian trade.

The relationship between Greek and Achaemenid sculpture and the practical continuity of Achaemenid and East Greek jewellery have already been mentioned, but it must be stressed that the Persian spoils in Athens captured from Mardonius, housed in the Parthenon and paraded at the Panathenaic festivals, must have had a formative influence on Greek taste. The captured Persian rhyta and other vessels had a direct influence on Greek pottery and metalwork, but this direct influence was brief, and it was probably the craftsmanship and sumptuousness of the spoils that was admired rather than their style; and so it most probably was with the Persian rugs and textiles which reached the west. The Scythian burials at Pasyryk in the Altai have preserved pieces of Achaemenid carpets with rows of grazing stags, fan-maned lion heads and filling rosettes. The coloured ceramic procession of the Immortals from the walls of the palace at Susa gives us another vivid glimpse of textile art, for the fabric of each guardsman's dress has an all-over pattern of woven castles. This small detail is not without interest; not only do numerous tablets from Susa deal with the weaving of coloured and embroided clothes and dresses but there is a Classical tale that a young dandy of Sybaris, vulgar-rich, wore a *himation* fifteen ells long entirely covered with mythological figures and representations of himself and of Persepolis and Susa.

Fig. 46

CHAPTER VII

From the Satrapies

OUR KNOWLEDGE OF THE everyday material culture of the Achaemenids is poor. A village at Susa, a short distance from the royal palace, is our only detailed source of vernacular building styles. The method of building houses in family blocks appears first in the Aryan homeland of Choresmia and it is to this region that the pottery of the village's earliest phase in part relates. Achaemenid pottery is, however, almost uniformly dull and at its best is a continuation of the metallic shapes of Assyrian pottery. The advent of the Persians did not change the local styles of pottery in use throughout the Near East, for the Achaemenids were not colonisers; but pottery which can be assigned to Achaemenid manufacture has been found in a few places outside Iran: Ur, Nippur, Tell Deim in Iraqi Kurdistan and Gordium in Phrygia.

It is thus from garrison-forts, treasure hoards, burials of officials and a few exports that we learn most about the Achaemenids abroad. Palaces of Persian style have been found at Sidon in Phoenicia and at Sar Tepe in Russian Azerbaijan, and stout official 'residences', planned on the Assyrian open-court palace, have been found at Tell Deim, Lachish and Tell Qasile in Palestine; doubtless many others existed. Achaemenid life in Asia Minor, the most important satrapy, was subject to overpowering Ionian, Lydian and Phrygian influences. A building recently excavated at Dascylium (modern Ergili) in north-west Anatolia was in all probability the residence of the satrap of Hellespontine Phrygia (Tyaiy drayahya), but despite the large numbers of purely Achaemenid clay bullae the building is as purely Ionic as are those of Sardis. Even the extensively built and fortified Persian level at Gordium, on the royal road from Ephesus to Susa, makes few concessions to Persian construction. But here and there relief sculpture of the late fifth century has both theme and treatment derived from Persia. Two isolated reliefs, one from Bünyan near Kayseri and the other from Dascylium, are purely Persian and show Median *Fig. 52* Magi, their loose fur coats thrown over their shoulders, in the act of performing sacrifices. Also from the Dascylium area is a frieze of horsewomen of a mixed Greco-Persian style. Other sculptured reliefs, particularly the rich series from the Nereid monument at Xanthos in Lycia, show Persian influence but to a much less marked degree. Apart from typically Achae-menid jewellery, such as that from Sardis and the silver plate *Plate 54* from Sinope, the products of the Ionian jeweller indicate that same Persian influence found amongst the Greeks of the south Russian colonies.

Naturally it was to the Scythians that Achaemenid objects had greatest appeal. The dinner services, upholstered beds and thrones designed for the mess tents of Persian officers on field duty admirably suited the taste of the covetous and pretentious nomadic Scythian leaders. Scythian tombs were elaborately furnished and, in any case, the Scythians not only had a close relationship with the Medes and Persians but supplied from their Ural territories much of the gold on which Persia de-pended. Numerous isolated Achaemenid objects have come *Plates 55, 57, 62* from Scythian tombs, both typical Achaemenid pieces like the rhyton from Kul Oba and those with a certain classical influence like the long curved fifth-century drinking horns (one with an unusual dog's-head terminal) from the Seven Brothers tumulus (Koban).

Scythian connexions with 'Median' art have been noticed in certain pieces of the Ziwiyeh treasure where animals of purely Scythian style are associated with animals of an Assy-rian-Urartian combination. Slightly later than this Scythian impact on Iran, influences from Median and Urartian sources travelled back to south Russia and are found in silver objects

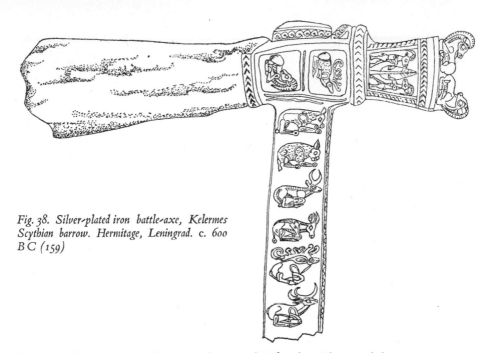

Fig. 38. Silver-plated iron battle-axe, Kelermes Scythian barrow. Hermitage, Leningrad. c. 600 BC (159)

from the burial mounds at Kelermes (Koban), Chertomlyk (Dniepr region) and Litoj (Kiev). Like plaques with lattice-tress patterns previously mentioned (p. 40), these pieces must now be regarded as belonging to a northern branch of Median art able to synthesize Urartian, Caspian and Scythian motifs. Certain aspects of this synthesis are to be seen at Ziwiyeh, evolving the style of material found in these earliest Scythian burials, particularly at Kelermes and the Litoj barrow.

The material from the Kelermes kurgan is the most important. Whilst not a tomb-group in the strictest sense, a silver mirror and a rhyton horn are Ionian Greek, probably products of some early Black Sea colony in Colchis, permitting a fairly close dating. Their attractive designs compare with painted Greek vases of about 600 BC and thus set the chronological framework for the Scytho-Median finds. Chief of these is an *akinakes* (the short Median sword of the Persepolis reliefs) and an iron-bladed battle-axe with a long silver shaft, a weapon

Fig. 38

137

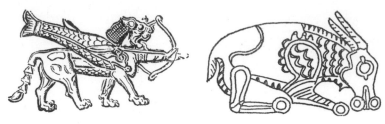

Fig. 39. Medo-Scythian animals: lion from a silver scabbard, Litoj kurgan; hare from an axe-foil, Kelermes. c. 600 B C (159)

regarded by Herodotus as peculiar to the Scythians, and carried by the Medians and Scyths at Persepolis. Although the sword blade has perished, the silver hilt and scabbard sheath are well preserved. The scabbard top and lower hilt both have an identical scene of Urartian origin: winged human genii plucking fruits from a sacred tree. The rest of the hilt is covered with a rather geometric sacred-tree design based on the geometric version of the Urartian tree pattern seen on the Fars and Karmir Blur plaques.

Fig. 39

The rest of the sheath, apart from the opposed lions of the chape, is occupied by a procession of mythical monsters (lion-griffins, lion-bulls, etc.) whose stylistic origins are to be found in the Ziwiyeh 'Median' plaques. One curious and hitherto unexplained addition is, however, the huge carp which lies along the back of every animal and appears to bite the front haunches. Certain priests in Assyrian reliefs often wear carp-skin hoods, but here on the Kelermes scabbard the fish appear to be alive. The protruding hand-guard on the top of the scabbard is purely Scythian, bearing a fine example of the Scythian royal stag within a border of griffin beaks stylised to make a sort of cable design. This appears to be a feature of early Scythian material and derives from the use of griffin heads as border designs at Ziwiyeh.

The crouched Scythian stag is found also on the shaft-hole of the battle-axe and in the vertical row of animals on the handle. These animals include goat, ibex, wild horse, ass, boar, antelope. Their feet are either naturalistically drawn or terminate in circlets or in small griffin heads, a Scythian peculiarity. The stylisation, the outstretched necks and internal body designs are certainly not in themselves Scythian, but rather derive from an animal tradition found on some of the Marlik Tepe beakers. Finally, attention should be drawn to a fine gold bowl with repoussé animal friezes, ostriches on top, goats, ibex and lion below, all in a style somewhat more Assyrian than those of the scabbard. Incidentally, ostriches seem to have been quite well known to the Urartians and Medians and even the Greek rhyton of Kelermes carefully distinguishes between ostriches and cranes. A second golden bowl is covered with pyramids in high relief and obviously copies a gadrooned bowl of Hamadan type. There are also curious ornaments ending in typically Urartian lion-heads.

Fig. 10c

The most important object from the Litoj treasure is a sword and scabbard almost identical with that of Kelermes and certainly from the same workshop. The pommels of both the Kelermes and the Litoj sword, as well as the chape of a sword of remarkably Assyrian shape from Shumeikos in the Poltava district, are decorated with gold granules, a technique rare in Scythia but now known in Urartu and Media. The chieftain was laid to rest in the Litoj barrow on a couch whose silver legs (of Assyrian-derived type) have survived. A barrow at Kalitva on the Don yielded a bronze bull's head of a type shown on relief representations of Assyrian and Urartian thrones.

The Chertomlyk barrow was a complex of burials of various dates. In one of those chambers was preserved a golden dagger hilt which is topped by a pommel of addorsed calves' heads, Achaemenid style. The rest of the hilt is occupied by a hunting scene, trousered horsemen hunting down wild goats with bow and arrow, strongly recalling a scabbard from the Oxus treasure.

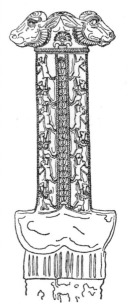

Fig. 40. Gold dagger-hilt, Chertomlyk barrow. Sixth century B C. Height 6 in. (155, 159)

This treasure is the most diversified and largest find of Achaemenid remains. It was in fact found in Bactria, not in Scythia proper, but the figures portrayed are mostly trousered Scythians. Discovered in 1877 in a sandy bank of the Oxus near Kunduz, the objects were traded first to Kabul and then to Peshawar before reaching the British Museum.

The Oxus jewellery shows a number of strains. Plaques and finial ornaments have a Scythian cast and a number of the plaques show Scythians dressed in their typical costume as on Persepolis reliefs and the Greco-Scythian metal vases from south Russia. A number of statuettes portray Medes in domed caps, heavy wool-lined sleeved coats and 'Balaclava helmets'. Two of them are placed in a golden chariot of the typical Persian box-cart type with great studded wheels, one of the greatest treasures of the British Museum. The other objects are of diverse dates and influences, but it is of great interest that Egyptian themes are represented by roundels of the god Bes and the Horus hawk. Standing out from this predominantly fifth-century material is a golden scabbard-sheath in shape like those from Kelermes and Litoj. It is embossed along its length with the scene of a royal lion-hunt in a style reminiscent of the reliefs of Assurbanipal's palace, except that the figures wear Scythian trousers and either Scythian caps or what looks like a version of the Assyrian royal crown. A somewhat similar hunt, for goats not lions, is seen on the hilt of the Chertomlyk dagger and it may be supposed therefore that in the early sixth century, when these pieces were made, the Medes still employed a theme they had copied from the palaces of Assyria.

Next in magnificence to the Oxus treasure is the less-known treasure from Achalgori in Georgia. Like the Oxus treasure it was found on a river-bank, but there are grounds for believing that it comes from a tumulus situated on the banks of the Ksanik river near the village of Sadseguri. The peasants who found it thought it was a cache of local church-plate, but

Figs. 41, 42

Fig. 41. *Gold figure of a Persian from the Oxus treasure. British Museum. Height 2½ in. (124)*

Fig. 42. One of a pair of inlaid gold armlets from the Oxus treasure. Victoria and Albert Museum. Diameter 4¾ in. Fifth century B C (123, 124)

gradually the pieces were collected and sold to the Tiflis Museum, in the province of which Achalgori lies. It seems to have been a burial in the grand Scythian manner in which the chieftain was accompanied in death, as at Kostromskaya and other great tumuli, by his horses. The numerous horse bits and other minor trappings are of Scythian-related style, but there is little in the magnificent gold-work which relates to Scythian art as we normally conceive it. Four flat gadrooned serving dishes are of Achaemenid make as are a number of the earrings and other pieces of jewellery. It is possible that a group of medallions belongs to a second and later strain of Medo-Scythian art and one to which we should assign the gold rhyton mounts of triangular shape both from Achalgori and

Fig. 43

Fig. 44

Fig. 45

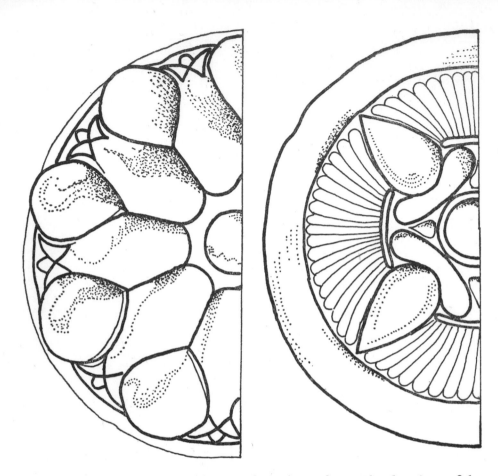

the Seven Brothers tomb in the Koban. The drawings of the wings and bar-tails of the birds on the Seven Brothers mounts has something in common with the Achalgori and Oxus dia-dem birds. The Achalgori rhyton mounts are covered with the same miniature palm trees as appear on the medallions. These are not normal Achaemenid palms, nor are the animal combats on the Seven Brothers mounts, so frequently described as Assyro-Persian, either Achaemenid or Assyrian. We can only assume that there existed in the early fifth century BC a Medo-Scythian style to the periphery of which these objects belong.

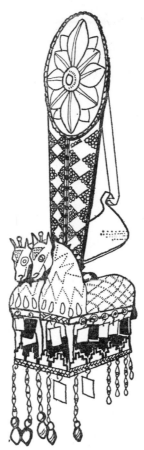

Fig. 43. (Opposite) Silver paterae with em-bossed designs found at Achalgori, S. Russia. Diameters 6¼ and 7½ in. (8, 161)

Fig. 44. Gold ear pendants from the Achalgori Treasure, S. Russia. Heights 1½ and 5⅛ in. (161)

Achaemenid objects found their way even farther afield in Russia. Scythian burials at Prokhorova in the Orenburg region (Urals) contained finely worked rugs, Achaemenid silver drinking bowls (two with Aramaic inscriptions) and an Achaemenid seal. One of the finest examples of a ram-headed beaker is the silver vessel discovered in 1734 at Usta Kamenogorsk in Siberia, now in the Hermitage. Another piece of remarkable silverware comes from Kazbekistan, a *phiale* embossed with palmettes between curved swan-necks identical with a bowl from a Greek grave in Rhodes. These

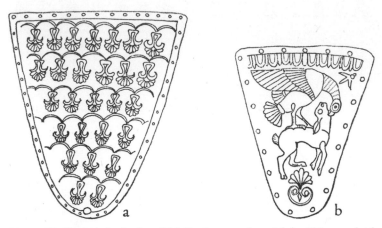

Fig. 45. Gold mounts for the lips of drinking horns: a, from Achalgori Treasure, height 4 in.; b, from the Seven Brothers tumulus, Koban, height 3½ in. (159, 161)

are but a selection; even without them there is enough intrinsic evidence to establish that such imports had a profound effect on Scythian arts and crafts in many media. The wooden fretwork, leatherwork and embroidery of the great frozen Scythian burials in the Altai, animal combats, swan-heads and-palmettes, the head of Bes and other themes, can have been adopted in such a remote region only from Achaemenid sources, and the preservation of fifth-century Persian rugs in the Pasyryk burial clearly demonstrates direct contact. A small but very significant detail is that the circle-and-drop treatment of the musculature of rumps, prevalent in Achaemenid fifth-century drawing, occurs on the animals of Altai-Scythian art.

Among the Thracians of Persia's only European satrapy of Skudra (Thrace, stretching into northern Bulgaria) Achaemenid taste had time to make a brief impact. The area has produced two Achaemenid finds which are probably of a fifth-century date. The first is possibly from Xerxes' time; it is a fine handle-spouted amphora of silver from the Kukova tumulus at Duvanlij near Plovdiv. The body is delicately

Fig. 46

Fig. 47

Fig. 46. Fragments of multicoloured woven braids from Scythian barrows, Altai; stag about 5 in., lions about 1½ in. long (160)

fluted and the shoulder decorated with a floret-and-bud chain. The Greek pottery dates the tumulus to the mid-fifth century, but the amphora was probably made half a century earlier; its handles in the form of winged lions with ibex horns have many archaic features closely comparable, especially in the manes, to a Metropolitan Museum rhyton, though the hind-quarters are outlined with a circle-and-drop motif characteristic of the fifth century, and the body of the vase is close in style to that of the Sinope base-spouted amphora (see p. 125). Again, from the Greek contents of the tomb in which they were found, two silver beakers and a cup from a chieftain's grave at Dolboki near Stara Zagora in east-central Bulgaria must be assigned to the second half of the fifth century. The cup is undecorated, but the conical beakers have a simple yet pleasing design of lotus-and-palm chain below the rim. It is interesting to note that the design round the lower parts of these beakers is derived from the coarse scale-like feathers found on Assyrian and Urartian beasts and used by the Achaemenids on such pieces as the Beyeler rhyton. This feather design was meaninglessly

Fig. 33

145

Plate 57

copied amongst the Scyths: we find it on one of the drinking horns from the Seven Brothers tumulus and also on Scythian armour and cheek-pieces of later date; it has a long survival in Scythian lands and appears on the famous Concesti amphora, Byzantine work of the fifth century A D.

In discussing these Achaemenid objects from Bulgaria, we must remember that Thrace was in contact with the Achae-menid world quite independently of the Persian satrapy there. Miletus had colonies on the western shore of the Black Sea and through the coastal carrying trade these were in close touch with such ports as Sinope. Although the Odrysian chieftains of Thrace imported goods from Athens, the same coastal trade brought work from Panticapaeum and other Crimean Greek centres, whilst the Scyths exerted a common influence on Crimean Greek and Thracian alike. Influences from all these sources are visible in the great gold find of 1949 at Panagjurishte near Plovdiv, belonging to the threshold of the Hellenistic era. The workmanship of the treasure is actually Greek; the animal-headed rhyta are close to the corresponding forms in Athenian pottery and are embossed with scenes from Greek mythology, but many small details of decoration, for instance the palmettes and the lion-spout on the base of one of the vessels, as well as a *phiale* with embossed negro-heads, are reminiscent of Greco-Scythian work. An amphora with handles in the shape of satyrs, although entirely Greek in decoration, is of the familiar Achaemenid shape. It is thought that the treasure was buried by an Odrysian chieftain during one of the Celtic invasions of Thrace in the second half of the fourth century B C.

Finds from the Levantine provinces are nowhere so rich. Damascus was, according to Strabo, the most important town of the Syrian region, but we know nothing about it under the Achaemenids. Among the Aramaeans of north Syria, at Neirab near Aleppo and Deve Hüyük to the north, there are

Fig. 47. Silver spout-handled amphora, Du-vanlij, Bulgaria. Height 10⅝ in. Fifth century B C (162)

important Achaemenid burials presumably belonging to garrison troops guarding official trade routes. The Neirab settlement appears to have been founded in the Neo-Babylonian period and to have continued into Achaemenid times, for clay cuneiform business documents found on the site can be dated back to the reigns of Nabonidus and Cambyses. The Deve Hüyük graves appear from the imported Cypriote and late Egyptian pottery to begin in the late sixth century and to continue into the fifth. The number of foreign objects buried with the soldiers and their women suggest that they had seen garrison duty in Egypt, Cyprus and Phoenicia. Besides weapons and horse bits of Irano-Scythian type, simple mirrors, fibulae and a set of metal tubes with lids, supposedly for kohl or some other cosmetic, were found. The settlements to which these graves belong have been little explored. The excavations at Neirab, Qadesh and Til Barsip have a further particular importance because of the Achaemenid terracotta figurines found there. Figures of women dressed in precisely similar clothing to that worn by Persian noblemen at Persepolis and holding the lotus in the breast position are our only indication of the outside copying of the Palace style. Also, securely dated at Neirab, is a group of terracotta models of horsemen. These were very popular in Palestine and Syria and even turn up in Persian Babylon. These little model Persian cavalrymen are useful 'type-fossils' of the 'Persian period' in regions where it is not archaeologically distinctive.

It is nowhere less distinctive than in dark Phoenicia. We may be sure that the commercial activities of the coastal cities were greatly increased under the Persians. Aradus, Byblos, Tyre and Sidon were autonomous states striking their own coinage, Aradus on the Persian standard, the others either on the Greek standard or Phoenician shekel. The dies of these coins were Greco-Phoenician, like those of the Persian standard coinage of the Cypriote cities, but Sidon, seat of the satrap, produced a beautiful shekel coinage stamped with a representation of a Persian ruler in a chariot and with a trireme on the reverse. Phoenicia's vital contribution to the empire was her fleet of 300 triremes, of which the king of Sidon was titular admiral. It made her a key factor in waging war and maintaining peace. It was probably for the High Admiral that a Persian-style palace was erected at Sidon. Little is known of it apart from the bull-capitals and globular bases now in the collection of the National Museum at Beirut, provincial imitations of the columns of Susa and Persepolis. But there are other indications that Sidon was now leader of Phoenicia: her coins and commercial amphorae penetrated Egypt and Persia, and Sidonians took up residence at Athens and on Rhodes. The local Phoenician kings, such as Tabnit and Eshmunazar, were elaborately buried in commodious Egyptian coffins of black granite and the Sidonian nobility in less expensive anthropoid sarcophagi, a considerable number of which have been found in the deep catacombs around the city. The great temple to Eshmun was rebuilt outside Sidon in the Persian period; there are signs of building at Aradus, Byblos and Tyre. But as regards Achaemenid art, we must remember that much of the trading population of the Phoenician cities was Greek, and that native taste looked to the Mediterranean rather than to that Asiatic hinterland with which it had had unhappy historical associations. A few pieces of sculpture, a pair of lions from the Baalat Gebel temple at Byblos, and some grave stelae from the area around Tyre show a degree of Achaemenid influence; but for the rest, outworn Egyptian themes, with some minor modifications in the Greek style, represent the limit of Phoenician aspirations.

Inland, the Persian province of Judah (*Yehud,* as it is called in the book of Ezra) had some administrative and fiscal independence of the Syrian-Babylonian satrapy. From Greek prototypes coins were first struck in Judah under the Persian regime, and the 'Persian period' is perhaps still best demarcated archaeologically by imported Attic pottery. It is, however, increasingly well known for the large number of storage-jar handles stamped with rather neutral designs of winged scrolls and flying birds, and the Hebrew letters *Yhd* (Yehud). It appears from Nehemiah that the expenses of the Persian administration were paid for by levies in cash and kind; it is probable that the stamped jars were a government issue intended to carry the levy of produce to certain provincial collecting centres. The distribution of these jars neatly defines what we know from Biblical sources to have been the Perso-Judaean province – Tell en-Nasbeh (Mispah, according to Nehemiah, a Persian administrative centre), Ramat Rachel, Jerusalem, Jericho, Gibeon, Lachish, Gezer. Many of these are the cities listed by Nehemiah as having contributed to the rebuilding of the walls of Jerusalem. Apart from the Lachish residency, no Persian level of any wealth has been found at any of these sites; after the Exile the country was poor and underpopulated. A seal impression from Gibeon, still bearing the imprint of the linen envelope of the document which it sealed, is one of the few Achaemenid objects found in Palestine.

To the south of Judah lay the important Arabia-Gaza lifeline, important not only because access to Egypt lay across it but also because it was the sea-outlet of the powerful Idumaean, Nabataean and Qedarite Arab states, which since Nabonidus' day had played an important part in Mesopotamian and Egyptian relations. To maintain an equilibrium of interests, Persians garrisoned the area and were installed at Aqabah. The Persian residency at Lachish was on the edge of Idumaean territory, and wealthy burials at Beth Pelet and Gezer attest the presence of officials there. A 'Persian fortress' discovered by Flinders Petrie at Tell Jemmeh (Gerar) is, however, not well substantiated. The burial of a governor or garrison commander in Petrie's Tomb 650 at Beth Pelet provides impressive evidence of Persian pomp. It contained a complete silver couch with six spooled legs and cross-pieces, silver fluted *phialae* and a delightful ladle whose handle is formed after the Egyptian pattern of a naked swimming girl, who holds the bowl of the ladle in her outstretched arms. The objects from Beth Pelet show points of particular interest: letters inscribed on the legs of the couch indicating how to piece the joints together are in Hebrew-Aramaic script, whilst the head of the swimming girl on the ladle is distinctly Semitic. They seem therefore to be products of a Syro-Palestinian workshop.

Fig. 48

The group of inscriptions from Tell el-Maskhuta, twelve miles west of Ismailia in Lower Egypt, must also have belonged to the commanders of garrison soldiers. They dedicated at a local desert shrine some silver bowls of normal Achaemenid type, but with Egyptian overtones which stamp them as local products. The find is a chance one, but from the same site come a number of Attic coins, some cat's-eye beads and boomerang-shaped pieces of agate in gold mounts of a type

Fig. 48. Bronze fittings for couch-legs and part of a silver wine service with drinking bowl and ladle (two views) from an Achaemenid grave at Beth Pelet, S. Palestine. Palestine Museum. Not to scale (152, 154)

found on other Achaemenid sites. A number of the bowls bear dedicatory Aramaic inscriptions to *Han 'Ilat*, a pre-Islamic goddess of the north Arabians and include one dedicated by 'Qainu son of Geshem King of Qedar'. He is possibly 'Geshem the Arabian' of the book of Nehemiah, who must have ruled the Qedarite tribes in north Arabia about 400 BC. It is known from Assyrian annals that from the early seventh century the Qedarites held supremacy amongst the Arabians.

We are also told by Herodotus that when Cambyses conquered Egypt in 525 BC, he had Arab aid. Possibly about
that time Qedarite tribes were allowed to settle in north-east
Egypt to guard the south Palestinian border and form a pro-
Persian buffer between the two lands. Certainly it was this
Ismailia-Port Said region that was known to the compilers of
Exodus as the 'Land of Goshen' (= Geshem). The names of the
persons dedicating these bowls show that a certain assimilation
of culture had taken place, since one bears a half-Egyptian,
another a fully Egyptian name. But apart from this, the find-
ing of Attic coins stamped with the head of Athena bears out
a suggestion made by Herodotus that the Arabians identified
her with their native goddess *Alilat*. Probably at Daphnae or
Naucratis, both Greek colonies near by, the Tell el-Maskhuta
settlers became familiar with Athena.

The Egyptians above all others constantly struggled to rid
themselves of Persian domination. Egypt had little to learn
from Persia and, whilst many Egyptian ideas and motifs
(e.g. cornices and glazed tile-work) were adopted for use in the
Persian palaces, Persian influence on XXVII Dynasty art
is small and confined to sculpture. Achaemenid delineation is
seen on a series of small carved rampant lions (a motif hitherto
unknown in Egypt) from Tell el-Muqdam, the site of the
temples of the lion-god Mahes at Leontopolis. The rump
muscles are cut away in circle-and-drop form to take inlay.
Glazed tiles from Koptos and Qantir appear closely related in

Plate 63

technique and glaze to tiles with Horus hawks from Persepolis.
A few objects appear to be exports from the Persian homeland:
a stone amulet in the Brooklyn Museum, with addorsed ram's
and lion heads, a wooden *akinakes* scabbard in the British
Museum and an interesting limestone plaque carved with
three rows of Achaemenid animals, said to be a gold-workers'

Plate 64

trial-piece or die.

If the provenance of this latter piece is secure, it provides additional evidence for the interchange of goldsmiths between Egypt and Persia. Reference has already been made to the collection of fluted and lotus-embossed metal bowls from Thmouis (Tell Tmai in the Delta) and their relationship to Achaemenid silverware. From their deep shapes they should be earlier than the reign of Xerxes. Important evidence for the manufacture of Achaemenid objects in Egypt comes from the wall paintings from the tomb of Petosiris (an official of Artaxerxes III's reign) at Tunah el-Gebel, which show the inside of a metalsmith's workshop. Overseers, dressed in the loose-sleeved jacket and long skirt typical of the XXVII Dynasty inspect the work of craftsmen who are producing rhyta, ladles, flat-rimmed paterae and animal-handled amphorae in pure Achaemenid style. We have no information about the situation of this workshop or whether it is strictly contemporary with Petosiris, who died a little before 300 BC. It is possible that the design came from an earlier painter's pattern book, but it at least provides excellent evidence for the existence of quite large-scale silverware factories. In respect of work in alabaster, we might even speak of 'mass-production', for over thirty alabaster bottles bearing the names of Xerxes and Artaxerxes in hieroglyphs and cuneiform are known. They were probably the ancient equivalent of our coronation mugs.

The part played by the Egyptian official, Udjahorresne, in the conquest of Cambyses and during the subsequent reign of Darius has already been described. Although he was strongly pro-Persian, nothing about his statue, except possibly his lion-head bracelets, suggests an admiration for Achaemenid art. This situation is reversed on the important inscribed statue of Ptah-hotep now in the Brooklyn Museum, one of the very rare Egyptian statues of the XXVII Dynasty. Whilst the long inscription on the back of the statue is entirely non-committal as to the part he played in the politics of the day and is merely an enumeration of his offices and good works, his costume and

Plates 47, 48

ornaments reveal his sympathies. Ptah-hotep is dressed in two plain garments: a long wrap-around skirt which covers his body from the breast to the ankles and is fastened at one side; under this he wears a close-fitting jacket with long flaring sleeves, the type of jacket worn by Persians in the Persepolis reliefs. Tailored clothing had never before been worn in Egypt, and representations of this jacket appear to be confined to statuary of the XXVII Dynasty; we have already noticed it in Petosiris' tomb. There are good grounds, therefore, for regarding it as a Persian introduction. Around his neck, Ptah-hotep wears, besides a usual type of Egyptian pectoral, an excellent Achaemenid torque terminating in crouched goats.

Ptah-hotep's inscription indicates his importance: 'The prince and count, royal treasurer and sole friend, one great in office and great in merit, the superintendent of all royal works, the minister of finance.' Despite his importance, he is known by only one other monument, a stela in the Louvre dated to the thirty-fourth year of Darius I and found at Memphis, where, the inscription records, Ptah-hotep had erected a monument.

Lower Egypt's Memphis, known to the Greeks as the 'White Castle', was made the administrative capital under Cambyses, and the presence there during the Persian domination of camps of mercenaries and foreign workmen, including shipwrights (for Memphis had always been a shipyard) is known not only from Herodotus' account but also from graffiti and grave-stones found at the site. According to Herodotus, camps for 'Jews' and 'Tyrians' as well as for Persians were established there; Aramaic and Phoenician graffiti have been found scratched on the fallen monuments of earlier dynasties, and Petrie discovered numerous impressions of Achaemenid seals and terracotta figures of foreigners, Semitics and Aegeans.

One of the most curious monuments from Memphis is a carved representation, once in Berlin, of the funeral rites of a

Median or Persian noble. The body is laid out upon a deep⁄ Plate 52
cushioned couch. Both this couch and the side table in front
of it belong to the Assyrian or Achaemenid style of furnishings.
The body has the curled beard and hair of an Assyrian or
Persian, but the sleeved garment he wears as well as the high
round⁄topped hat suggest the Median dress as seen in the
Persepolis reliefs. No less interesting are the figures which
accompany the lying⁄in⁄state. Two women who stand at the
head of the couch have torn the garments from their breasts
and are tearing their hair. They are probably hired Egyptian pro⁄
fessional mourners. But the two male figures at the foot of the
couch wear trousers and knee⁄length surcoats, and hats of the
same shape as those of the deceased. These surely must be
the Medes or Scyths. Furthermore, in the background of the
scene a groom stands with a horse, probably the deceased's
mount which either is intended for inclusion in the tomb, as
was the Scythian custom, or is here appearing shorn of its
mane as a sign of mourning.

Without including in this brief survey the sporadic finds of
Achaemenid objects, such as a bowl from Athens, a bracelet
from Corinth, and model silver mountain sheep from India, it Plate 72
will be appreciated that the material is widely distributed and
patchy. Disappointing though this may be, it is a fact of some
importance. Unlike Mycenae in Bronze Age times, unlike
the land of Assur in the Assyrian Empire and Athens in the
Delian League, the Persian homeland of Fars, although the
local centre of Achaemenid art and aspirations, provided no
economic or trade centre for the conquered lands. It was
relatively unsettled, underpopulated and undeveloped, and
furthermore lay off the well⁄beaten tracks of Mesopotamian⁄
Syrian trade routes. Persia proper was scarcely known to the
Greeks.

CHAPTER VIII

The Later History

THE BITTER FRUITS of Xerxes' short-sighted policy in
Egypt were soon to be tasted by his son, Artaxerxes I.
The trouble came from Inarus, a son of an ex-pharaoh and
a Libyan, who opportunely visited Pericles in Athens in
460 BC seeking aid against their mutual enemy. The Greeks
had not capitalised on their sweeping victory at the Eurymedon.
The fleet of the Delian League was able to control the Levant
and, under Cimon, even to attempt the reconquest of Cyprus;
but Corinth and Aegina were locked in a private war, and the
former allies of mainland Greece were thus disunited. But now
an Athenian army embarked for Egypt, killed Achaemenes
the satrap and captured Memphis. Had this expedition succeeded in establishing the independence of Egypt, Persia
would have suffered her greatest blow, but it ended in complete disaster for Athens and turned her thoughts to peace.
A delegation led by Callias, Athens' ablest diplomat, was
sent to Susa to negotiate the terms. Persia recognised the
supremacy of Athens over those Ionian states in the Delian
League and prepared to grant autonomy to those remaining
in vassalage to the Great King. No Persian ships were to
sail into the Aegean or the Propontis and no satrapal troops
were to approach within fifty miles of those parts of coastal
Asia Minor controlled by Athens. For her part, Athens
abandoned Cyprus and interference in Egypt and probably
agreed to demilitarise Ionia.

Artaxerxes now used his completely free hand to consolidate
the position of Egypt under the new satrap Arsames. Megabyzus had given Inarus and the other leaders of the Egyptian
rebellion a safe-conduct to the court at Susa, but Artaxerxes,
it is said, violated it at the instigation of the queen mother,

a   b

Fig. 49. Impressions of cylinder seals: a, seal of Darius I with trilingual inscription, British Museum. Height $1\frac{1}{3}$ in.; b, Artaxerxes I slays the Egyptian rebel Inarus (?) Seal in the Hermitage, Leningrad Height $1\frac{1}{10}$ in. (102, 103)

Amestris, and slew them. The scene of execution is depicted on an Achaemenid cylinder seal. It was almost certainly this act of treachery that prompted Megabyzus to organise a revolt in Syria, for he is presented to us as a man of singular ability and integrity. This event underlines the besetting weaknesses of Achaemenid rule – the influence of royal women in affairs of state and how time after time they managed to alienate the ablest generals.

Fig. 49b

The conditions laid down by the Peace of Callias for the settlement in Ionia were scarcely likely to be observed for long. Throughout the archonship of Pericles, Athens pursued a policy friendly to Persia, and Zopyrus, the son of Megabyzus, whose name was held in gratitude by the Athenians for his leniency to the captured Greek generals in Egypt, was well received in Athens in 445. There he met Herodotus, 'Father of History', who was undoubtedly ready to supplement the reminiscences of his own recent travels in Asia with some 'official' tales of Achaemenid history. Soon a state of open war between the Ionians and Pissuthnes, satrap of Sardis, who had won back the allegiance of many of the Athenian cities, showed that the Peace was nothing but a cease-fire, and matters might once more have come to a head if the Peloponnesian war between Athens and Sparta had not broken out in 431, engaging the total energies of the two leading Greek states. In the first round, Persia did not intervene. The energies of Artaxerxes I were beginning to ebb. He died in 425 on the same day as his wife, Damaspia.

Their son, Xerxes II, ruled for but forty days. His murder by his half-brother, Secydanius, son of Artaxerxes by a Babylonian concubine, started a chain of gruesome events. Scarcely had the murderer seized the throne than Ochus, a third son of Artaxerxes, likewise by a Babylonian concubine, raised revolt in Babylon, where Artaxerxes I had made him satrap. Hyrcania, his earlier satrapy, declared for him, and Arsames supported him from Egypt. In 423 he was declared king of Babylon with the title Darius (II). His first act was to purge the palace: Secydanius and all those connected with the murder of Xerxes were put to death.

The Persians had been in no position during the first phase of the Peloponnesian war to take advantage of the Greek split. To the insecurity of Persia's internal affairs must be added the refractory attitude of satrap Pissuthnes in Sardis. In the second phase of the war (after the 'Peace of Nicias', 421–414) Sparta could not afford to miss the opportunity afforded by the plight of the Athenian allies in Asia Minor. In order to bring Pissuthnes to subjection Persia had despatched Tissaphernes, an able politician and sly statesman, the very gift to Sparta's intrigues. Tissaphernes' money soon robbed Pissuthnes of that Greek mercenary aid on which his truculence depended, and soon he himself was captured and executed as a rebel. By occupying the Carian coast with Athenian aid, Amorges, Pissuthnes' son, provided the necessary excuse for the Great King to enter the war formally on Sparta's side. Amorges was defeated and his troops accepted service under Tissaphernes. Separately the many mainland members of the Delian League accepted Persian garrisons and switched tribute. Between them Pharnabazus, satrap of Dascylium, and Tissaphernes, now in the position of Supreme Military Governor,

Fig. 50. Persians fight Thracians: impression of a cylinder seal in the British Museum. Fourth century B C (102)

had brought all the Greeks in Asia Minor under Persian rule. Indirectly, Persia won the Peloponnesian war for Sparta.

As so often in Persian history, successes were offset by trouble in Egypt. Cyprus too was in an equivocal position, for there a Phoenician local ruler had in 411 gained control of the Phoenician colonies at Citium and Idalium and was flouting Persia with pro-Athenian politics. Phoenicia herself was concerned about him. The trouble in Egypt broke in the following year with the revolt of Vidarnag, the commander-in-chief in Libya. The occasion was the absence of satrap Arsames on a duty visit at Susa. The causes and courses of the revolt are unknown to us, except that in 405 it was joined by Amyrtaeus, a second Egyptian pretender of that name, who gained sway in the delta and the Nile valley; but the events of these years are brought sharply into focus by accidents of survival, for two groups of contemporary Aramaic papyri shed valuable sidelights on them.

No group of documents from Persian times has been of such wide interest as the Aramaic correspondence of the colony of exiled Jews at Elephantine (Jeb) on the Nile, 800 km. south of Cairo. Naturally it is to biblical scholarship that the contribution of these documents is greatest, but they shed valuable light on Persian administration in Egypt. Elephantine (named after the ivory trade) was an outpost, an island in mid-Nile on the borders of Ethiopia, whither Cambyses had not ventured. The Jews of the colony, or at least some of them, belonged to a *degel*, or company named after their Persian or Babylonian commanding officer. The other residents were wives and

families of attached personnel, drawing rations from the govern‐
ment and living in provided quarters.

Whilst the Jewish colony appeared content in its military
role and doubtless in the trading sidelines it offered, there was
a major clash with the native priests of the temple of the ram‐
god Khnoum, built on the island long before the settlers
arrived. The Jews had their own temple and altar of sacrifice
to Yahu (Yahweh), 'God of Heaven', as in Ezra and Nehemiah,
the only one we know to have existed outside Jerusalem.
The papyri letters tell how the priests of Khnoum had this
temple destroyed during the revolt of 410, and how the Jews
attempted to get it rebuilt by sending letters to high Persian
authorities in Egypt and Palestine, including Bagohi, the
Persian governor of Judaea, successor of Nehemiah. Amongst
the documents, besides business letters, marriage licences and
manuscripts of slaves, was a full Aramaic transcript of Darius'
Behistun inscription.

As Arsames was on leave at the time, the Jews addressed
their letters to Bagohi at Jerusalem and to the sons of Sanballat,
governor of Israel and Samaria. Johanan, the high priest at
Jerusalem, had, they complain, not answered their letters, but
contact was eventually made with Arsames himself and a new
petition went off to him. In the surviving copy the Elephantine
priests stipulate that no animals will be sacrificed in the temple,
only meal and drink. Were the Jews anxious not to offend
Arsames' Zoroastrian sensibilities by reminding him of their
contamination of fire by the burning of animal parts? More
likely it was the homeland Jews they were intent to placate,
since the purification and centralisation of Jewish religious
law brought about by Ezra and Nehemiah would not have
tolerated the unorthodoxy of regarding any place outside the
Jerusalem temple as the proper place for burnt offerings to
Yahweh. A further reflection of the centralisation of Jewish
law under the Persian regime and of Arsames' own grasp of

Jewish affairs is a letter from him dated before the destruction of the Elephantine temple, ordering the colonists to celebrate the Passover according to Pentateuchal Law. Not only are the absence of Arsames and the conditions of unruliness thus confirmed in the papyri, but the entry of Amyrtaeus is mentioned in Papyrus 35, which refers to him as king.

A more recently published group of Aramaic papyri from Elephantine, now in the Brooklyn Museum, takes the history of the colony a little further and shows that Persian rule continued in some form in Egypt down to the end of 402 BC under Artaxerxes II – the winter before the rebellion of Cyrus the Younger. It seems probable that Egypt shook off allegiance to Persia only when the revolt of Cyrus had started, since the Brooklyn papyri show that Elephantine still owed allegiance to Artaxerxes II in the winter preceding the *anabasis* in 401 BC. More important for the history of the Elephantine colony is a letter written about business affairs by Shewa bar Zachariah from somewhere in Egypt to his associate Yislah in Elephantine. In this he alludes to the capture of King Amyrtaeus and the accession of Nepherites I (398?), founder of the XXIX Dynasty at Memphis. The Hebrew colony had been treated well under Amyrtaeus, but the XXIX Dynasty was devoted to the ram-god Khnoum, whose temple at Elephantine was a thorn in the flesh to the worshippers of Yahweh. Previously they had sought to get rid of it without success. Now the rise of the new dynasty was their death-knell: we hear nothing more of them.

Arsames' interest in Egypt went deeper than politics: much of his money was entailed there. By curious chance some of his business correspondence was found in Egypt in a sealed leather diplomatic bag and acquired by the Bodleian Library, Oxford, in 1944. It comprises twelve complete letters and fragments written in official Aramaic on strips of leather parchment, including letters from Arsham (Arsames) to

Netihur, an Egyptian official charged with the control of Arsames' large personal estate in Lower Egypt. They deal with mundane matters: collection of revenues, transference of a father's revenues to his son who has succeeded him in office, a summons to appear before the satrap, release of soldiers wrongfully seized; one is a passport for Netihur. On internal evidence these letters must be regarded as mostly written by Arsames during his absence from Egypt in 411–410 BC. One speaks of his being back and another of troubles 'whilst we were away'. Add to this the statement in one of the Elephantine papyri that the local detachment of Egyptian troops had revolted 'in the fourteenth year of King Darius, when our lord Arsham went to the King', and we obtain remarkable evidence for the Egyptian revolt of 410.

The complicated manœuvres conducted by Tissaphernes and the Spartans in pursuance of the Greek war in the Aegean were soon to be taken out of his hands by the less public manœuvres of Queen Parysatis. On Darius' accession his eldest son Arsaces was formally declared heir. Parysatis hated him and schemed with all her powers to advance her second son Cyrus, the younger brother. In 407, when Cyrus was barely sixteen, she managed to arrange for him to relieve Tissaphernes of the high command in Asia Minor. She reasoned that since the bulk of the Persian forces were stationed in the west, he who commanded them could make himself king. Cyrus already behaved in Asia Minor with the lavishness of a king. Abandoning the sly tactics of Tissaphernes, who had continually used the Spartans as well as helped them, Cyrus was openly helpful. The finance he now provided aided the Spartans to win the battle of Aegospotami and so cut off from Athens her Russian grain supply. In 404 Athens was starved into surrender.

Darius himself was only distantly concerned in these events. Media revolted in this same year and Cyrus was called to join the home forces. Darius fell ill in the course of the campaign and was taken back to Babylon, where he died. Despite his mother's schemes, Arsames was declared king, assuming the title Artaxerxes II (404–359), but nicknamed Mnemon, 'The Memory Man', by the Greeks. He was weak, ever in the clutches of Parysatis or of his equally noxious wife Stateira. And if we may believe the memoirs of his Greek doctor, Ctesias, the intrigues of his household left him scarcely a dull moment.

Obviously Cyrus had to contest the throne with arms. Tissaphernes, relegated to the governorship of Caria, and Pharnabazus were both won over, with the result that he controlled the entire military resources of Asia Minor. Furthermore, there were plenty of Greek mercenaries unemployed because of the end of the Peloponnesian war. Xenophon the Athenian was among them. Syennesis, king of Cilicia, joined Cyrus, and the whole war-machine was assembled on the pretext of attacking tiny Pisidia. In 401 they marched to within sixty miles of Babylon and there at Cunaxa met the army of Artaxerxes and Abrocomas, satrap of Syria. The rebels were defeated, and Cyrus felled in a personal attack on his brother. The rest of the story is told by Xenophon in his account of how the ten thousand helpless Greeks struggled back from the heart of Mesopotamia to the sea at Trapezus.

The revolt of Cyrus was the greatest blow the Achaemenid line had ever to sustain. It not only demonstrated its degenerate internal strife, but set Persia on a downward path internationally; for Cyrus, though a rebel, was a significant and vital character in comparison with his brother Artaxerxes. Though young, he was experienced in Persia's most vital sphere in the west, and it speaks highly for him that both Pharnabazus and initially Tissaphernes joined his cause. Had he won the gamble, he might have put an end to the old Achaemenid mould of oriental ruler and brought the empire more in line with the realities of the times. Greece was not merely a political enemy but the single largest cultural factor in the Persian empire. Not only had Hellenism invaded Asia Minor, where the satraps were more and more adopting Greek dress and manners, and Greek along with native Lydian and Lycian had become common languages, but Egypt, Cyprus and Phoenicia were noticeably deeply drawn into the sphere of Greek thought in the first half of the fourth century. In the subsequent vicissitudes of Achaemenid history the crucial position of Asia Minor was never completely mastered by the Great Kings. Sparta's ingratitude in siding with Cyrus rather than with the Great King underlines the fact that she knew that in dealing with Asia Minor she was not in fact dealing directly with Persia at all. Only Tissaphernes knew the western situation intimately, and he, after his defeat at the hands of King Agesilaus of Sparta, fell victim to the liquidations of Parysatis.

Almost the entire reign of Artaxerxes II was drained by the war against the Cadusian tribes which broke out in his father's reign. He had no time for Asia Minor, and with Tissaphernes removed, the political upper hand which Persia had managed to hold throughout was brought low. On Artaxerxes' death in 358, the outer empire was almost fractured away. The tremendous energies of his son and successor, Artaxerxes III, 'Ochos' (358–338), whom we can truly claim as the last of the great rulers of the ancient Near East and the last Achaemenid of consequence, effected a final revival. His aim to reunify the empire began first with Syria and Phoenicia, whose unruliness was backed by a still independent Egypt. In defence of the regime of Necht-har-habi in Egypt, Egyptians and Greeks fought side by side, and it was not until 343 that Egypt was returned to satrapal status and savagely punished. Over the satraps and independent princelings of Asia Minor Artaxerxes III also eventually established control, but here the rise of the Macedonian kingdom had brought into the game a third party whose military powers and diplomatic craft equalled those of Greek and Persian alike. The achievement of Artaxerxes III was due to no historical advantages but rather to his unscrupulous and uncompromising character. He was a winner of wars, and it was the death-signal for the Achaemenid empire when the eunuch Bagoas poisoned him.

Whilst Bagoas played king-maker, placing Ochos' son Arses on the throne, King Philip of Macedon, who at the battle of Chaeronea in 338 had put an end to Greek inde-pendence and unified the Greek states behind him under the leadership of Corinth, was preparing the attack on Persia. In 336 a ten-thousand-strong army under marshals Attalus and Parmenion moved into Asia Minor to liberate the Greek-speaking states. This was the signal for Egypt to revolt. The quickly fading relationship between Bagoas and Arses resulted in the murder of Arses and his family. Bagoas offered the throne to Darius, great-nephew of Artaxerxes I, the only eligible scion of the Achaemenid house to have escaped the blood-baths of Bagoas and Artaxerxes III.

Darius III 'Kodomannos' (336–330) was the last Achae-menid. He had a spark from the family fire and was personally brave. Without trouble he reduced Egypt but he culpably ignored the Macedonian threat. In the year of his accession, Philip was murdered, and the Macedonian throne occupied by his dynamic twenty-year-old son, Alexander.

The troops of Persia's western command were scattered by Alexander on the river Granikos in the summer of 334. In the following year Darius marched westwards with the home command and was defeated by Alexander near Issos and fled, leaving his family as prisoners of war. Whilst Alexander conquered Egypt, Darius mustered a second force. On October 1, 331 on the plain of Erbil, over against Nineveh, whose ruins stood as a monument to the first great victory of the Achaemenid line under Cyrus I, the Achaemenid army in the splendour of the attire of its many component nations was drawn up for the last time. In the battle at near-by Gaugamela it was all but destroyed.

Gaugamela was not the end. Darius himself fled to the Caspian, only to be murdered a few days later by a relative named Bessos, who took the throne and called himself Artaxerxes. His prospects seemed good: east Iran was the Iranian stronghold and supplied the core of the Persian army; it was primitive, relatively peaceful and untroubled by strong nationalistic movements. But he could not prevail against Alexander and in 327 Artaxerxes IV, 'Bessos', fell to the conqueror.

Either as a drunken whim or as an act of cool revenge for the Persian burning of the Athenian acropolis, Alexander burned down the palace at Persepolis. Ironically, his flames preserved it for posterity: the massive timber, earth and tile roof collapsed, forming a protective cover for the stairs and sculptures and preserving the clay tablets of the Treasury. Time would have dealt more savagely than the conqueror's wrath. Although the administrative structure of the satrapies was retained by the new regime, the centres of Achaemenid life and culture died rapidly. In the division of the empire on Alexander's death in 323, the eastern province fell to his chief general, Seleucus, a man of mixed Iranian and Greek blood, who during Alexander's later years had been rewarded by appoint-ment as satrap of Babylon, now briefly reinstated as the capital of Mesopotamia and beyond. Soon, however, the eastern province of the Seleucid territories were to be governed from new cities which Seleucus founded and populated with Greek colonists. These were Antioch-on-Orontes and Sel-eucia on the Tigris.

The foundation of these cities was the beginning of a policy which was to Hellenize the whole of western Asia. It sought not only to spread that common denominator of culture which might ensure the Seleucid hold on racially diversified subjects and to remedy a conspicuous Achaemenid failing by fusing them into a whole, but also to satisfy the land-hungry demobilised soldiers, who had little hope of scratching a living in impoverished Macedonia and Greece. Unlike the Achaemenids, whose political concepts were essentially those of Assyria, the Greeks had long experience of colonisation. In the course of years of campaigning they had become aware of the potentialities of underdeveloped lands, and had recognised that the development of the trans-Asiatic trade routes to India and China would be a key factor in the economic life not only of the now populous Levantine cities but of the Mediterranean as a whole.

We have concentrated in these chapters on the artistic achievement of the Achaemenids and on the special quality of their civilisation in relation to their Median forebears. There can be little doubt that the outline given in this short space will be considerably filled out if the present rate of discovery and excavation in Iran and the rest of the Middle East is maintained. Not only will the material aspects of Achaemenid culture be greatly illuminated but there is fair hope that documents such as those recently discovered in the Wadi Daliyeh caves in Jordan will throw greater light on administration and politics in the provinces.

CHAPTER IX

The Pulse of Power

COMPARED WITH THE EARLIER EMPIRES of Egypt, Assyria and Babylonia, the Achaemenids were remarkably successful. The outstanding general reason must surely be that the Achaemenid attitude to power was entirely new and creative. Where the Assyrians had boasted of the yoke they had imposed and gloated over the tribute exacted, Cyrus views himself as a liberator, Darius and Xerxes as divinely chosen to rule and establish a new order. The atmosphere is more that of the Holy Roman Empire than of Augustan Rome. On the practical side, the economic facilities fostered by the new order were a major reason for success, frequently bringing about voluntary submission to Persian rule. The conquered lands were dominated but not exploited; natural economic units were left to function as before. Thus Phoenicia and Cilicia continued their crafts and trade, and in Mesopotamia numerous business documents show that the temples still functioned as banks and trading centres, as from Sumerian times. Under protection, sea and land traffic everywhere increased and the widespread use of coinage facilitated trade. More significant was Darius' standardisation of the value of precious metals in terms of degree of purity. Although the use of the Persian gold darics was not widespread and few of the coinages of the empire were issued on the Persian shekel standard, the 'king's measure' was everywhere recognised.

Fig. 51

Away from the centres of commerce, a new prosperity was brought to the countryside. The satraps apparently held considerable portions of crown lands for their own use, providing labour and capital for their development. Agriculture was held in high regard by the Persians themselves: their religious beliefs prevented spoliation of the countryside, as sum-

Fig. 51. a, *Lydian Coin from the Persepolis Treasury. b, Gold daric of Darius. c, Coin of Tissaphernes, Asia Minor. Enlarged*

marised by the words of Arsites, satrap of Dascylium: 'I will not stand by and see one farm burnt of those which the King has committed to my hands.' In all, the Persian nobility had a deep sense of responsibility not only for the physical protection of their provinces but also for the maintenance of law and order. The satrap was no regional dictator but was a member of a civil service, graded and departmentalised, through which he was expected to act.

It was Darius who established the rule of law. His inscriptions suggest that the role of Lawgiver was the one he most fancied. The Law Code which he promulgated was not new but consisted of the codification of Babylonian case laws or legal decisions which are referred to as *dat*, the same word used for divine order in the Avesta. Not a fragment of Darius' laws has survived, and the extent of their implementation in the various countries is unknown to us, but the 'Laws of the Medes and Persians' became a by-word of judicial incorruptibility – and harshness – throughout subject lands. Special courts existed with permanent judges, and the efficiency of legal administration was aided by *azdakara* or 'publicity officers', a royal mail system and the maintenance of good roads such as the famous trunk road from Sardis to Susa, recently traced. Royal inscriptions leave no doubt of the high-minded and religious attitude to power of the Achaemenid monarchs. Tolerance of foreign religions was one of the most enlightened features of *pax persica* and is documented by such events as Cyrus' restoration of Babylonian shrines and Yahweh's temple at Jerusalem, by Cambyses' dedication of an Apis bull at Memphis, and by the aid sought by Xerxes of Apollo at Branchidae.

The explanation does not lie in any documented universalism or syncretism on the part of the Achaemenids. Rather the tolerance was engendered by the native henotheism mixed with prudence. Nowhere is there evidence that they thought of Ahuramazda and Yahweh as manifestations of the same 'Lord God of Heaven'. Both Darius and Xerxes, in declaring their theocratic rule under Ahuramazda, are careful to add 'and the other gods that are'. Cyrus, too, in thanking the Babylonian deities for his victories, is willing to acknowledge their powers whilst under the tutelage of the omnipotence of Ahuramazda, The Wise Lord, 'greatest of the gods'.

The relationship between the Achaemenids (especially Darius I) and the prophet Zoroaster, who is now widely recognised to have lived shortly after 600 BC, has been much debated, and opposing conclusions arrived at. In their Mazdaism, dualism and terminology the inscriptions of Darius and Xerxes are reminiscent of the Avesta, the body of Old Persian literature preserved by the Parsees of India. Amongst the service-books, hymns and mythological material which make up the Avesta, a group of hymns called *gathas* are the oldest and, besides incorporating much biographical information about Zoroaster, are written in what seems the archaic dialect of Bactria or Choresmia where the prophet lived. Similarity between Darius' epitaph and the *gathas* led certain scholars to believe that he was actually quoting the Avesta, whilst the reconstructed Avestan biography led

Herzfeld and Olmstead to identify that king Gushtasp who was Zoroaster's first patron with Hystaspes, satrap of Parthia-Hyrcania and father of Darius. Thus implying that Darius had been influenced in boyhood by Zoroaster. Both these arguments must now be discounted. The archaic language of the *gathas* has been shown not to be identical with the Old Persian of the Achaemenid inscriptions, even if similar sentiments are expressed. Secondly, the identification of Gushtasp with the Achaemenid Hystaspes is most uncertain, since Gushtasp's descendants in the Avesta are unknown to Achaemenid history. Hutaosa, wife of Gushtasp and Zoroaster's first convert, cannot be that Atossa who was wife – not mother – of Darius the Great. None of the Achaemenids is mentioned in the Avesta. It is none the less apparent that Zoroaster and Darius were products of the same intellectual climate, though certainly of different social backgrounds.

Stouvé and other scholars argue that the Achaemenids and the Zoroastrians ignored one another, and that all reference to the west Iranian monarchs was expunged from the Avesta. Certainly Zoroaster's role as mediator between God and man and his claim to special election by Ahuramazda appear to be usurped by both Darius and Xerxes. An inscription of Xerxes' from Persepolis even goes so far as to claim that it was he who expelled from west Iran the cult of the *daevas*, the old Iranian sky and weather gods demoted by Zoroaster, and destroyed their temples. This 'daiva' inscription makes Xerxes assume the role of 'Saoshyant' or 'Saviour', the very function claimed for Zoroaster in the later Avesta, and the name of the 'deliverer' whose advent the Zoroastrians expected. If for this reason the Zoroastrians could not accept the Achaemenids, it is strange that the Avesta does not express disapproval, and still more surprising that Zoroaster remained unknown to the Classical commentators on Achaemenid history, namely Herodotus, Xenophon and Strabo. We should perhaps conclude that the Achaemenid kings performed for the western Aryans the same function as Zoroaster in the east of the country, both at entirely different social levels and without conflict. Both followed a dualistic pattern; in the Avesta Angra Mainyu (Ahriman, the wicked spirit) is opposed to Ahuramazda (later Ormuzd), whilst to Darius the opposing principles were *Arta*, divine order, and *Druj*, 'the Lie'.

How far can their similarity in terminology be the result of a common religious climate? Perhaps Achaemenid religion and Zoroastrianism can best be explained as parallel developments from a common source, the former lacking the strict monotheism of Zoroastrian Mazdaism as well as its refinement in liturgical practice. We should perhaps separate the Mazda worship instanced in the Median territories in the eighth century BC from the specifically ethical and universalistic Mazdaism preached by Zoroaster, recognition of

Fig. 52. Fire-altar with relief of a Magus, from Bünyan, Kayseri, Turkey

Fig. 53. Noble and Magus worship at twin fire-altars; relief on a tomb façade at Saka-vand, Kurdistan. Seventh-sixth centuries B C (5, 78)

which is rendered difficult by a cloak of folk religion thrown over it in the Avesta. Such a view calls in question the obscure role played by the Magi whose priestly function had its strongest impact in west Iran and east Anatolia, in regions which had been in contact with old Urartu-Parsua.

The Magi are one of five aboriginal Iranian tribes named by Herodotus and appear to have been a religious caste rather than a tribe proper. Three other tribes cannot be identified, but the Arizantoi (*Arya* and *zantu*, tribe) were probably the Aryans *par excellence*, amongst whom Mazda-worship took shape. At an early stage, whilst the Aryan Mazdaeans resided in Urartu-Media, their religion had been cloaked in Median magianism with its blood sacrifices, fire-worship, *haoma* rites and astrology. Meanwhile in east Iran Mazdaism had been purified by Zoroaster and, in reaction to the magianisation and the aristocratic ethos of the west, may have embodied the simple nomadic and democratic ideas of the east. This, of course, is conjecture. It can certainly be questioned whether Zoroaster did in fact totally repudiate magian practice, and it is equally possible that aspects of ethical Zoroastrianism entered west Iran through the Magi. In short, we are totally in the dark. All we can say is that the Magi, like the Achae-

Fig. 52

menids, are not mentioned in the Avesta. We must also stress that the Magi were essentially cult-priests, not theologians, and that their function was not *totally* incompatible with the religious beliefs of either Zoroaster or the Achaemenids.

Besides Mazda-worship and similar forms of dualistic expression, the Achaemenids and Zoroastrians both practised fire-worship. The Zoroastrian priests were called *athravan* or fire tenders, whilst the Magi seem to have been mainly sacrificial priests whose animal sacrifices, as described by Herodotus, were remarkably like those of the earlier Vedic Aryans. We cannot say precisely how fire-worship was related to Mazda-worship in either Zoroastrian or Achaemenid cult. In their tomb reliefs the Achaemenid monarchs stand in front of the fire-altar whilst Ahuramazda flies above. If we accept the arguments of Hinz that fire-cult is properly Zoroastrian, then we shall have to take these reliefs and the 'fire-towers' (for preserving the sacred flame) built at Pasargadae by Cyrus and at Naqsh-i Rustam by Darius (?) as unequivocal evidence that the Achaemenids were Zoroastrians. It is also possible to take into account here the implication that Darius repudiated the Magi, together with his claim to have rebuilt the sanctuaries which Gaumata the Magian had destroyed (Behistun inscription), as indicating that these were fire-temples to which the Magi were opposed. It is, however, from the reign of Xerxes, when the Magi were in favour with the Achaemenids, that the Zoroastrian calendar was adopted throughout Iran. This is the only concrete evidence of Achaemenids adopting Zoroastrian ideas. At variance with this is the evidence that the Achaemenid Persians buried their dead and did not practise exposure, as enjoined by Zoroaster, to prevent the pollution of the earth. It might be that magian influence and the recrudescence of pre-Zoroastrian religion eventually led to practices which were the antithesis of Zoroaster's precepts in many respects. Thus we find Xerxes sacrificing

Fig. 53

Plate 43

Fig. 54. Gold medallion and cylinder seal impression (Clercq Collection) showing Anahita. Medallion diameter about 1 in.; seal height 1⅛ in. Fifth century B C

bulls to Trojan Athena and the intoxicating liquor *haoma,* a cultic drink forbidden by Zoroaster, used, according to the evidence of tablets, at Persepolis.

Herodotus speaks with the surprise of a Greek when he notes that the Persians did not have statues of their gods. Whilst it is true that the Persians avoided erecting statues and temples, and used only the representation of Ahuramazda copied from the Assyrian god Assur, later events modify Herodotus' statement. In pre-Zoroastrian times Mithras the sun-god and Anahita the mother-goddess had been widely worshipped, and it is quite clear that the Medes had temples, for Sargon II and Shalmaneser III both took booty from them, including statuary. Berossus, the Babylonian Greek writer, records how Artaxerxes I had temples of Anahita erected in the provincial capitals. Since his inscriptions frequently invoke Anahita and Mithras together, there were possibly Mithras temples and statues also. Supporting this is the specific iconography in the Avestan *Mithra Yahst* where Mithras is described as a charioteer sun-god. In India by 250 B C the sun-god Suryas are shown as charioteers with additional details corresponding to the *Mithra Yahst.* But it is precarious to argue back from this that such a close link existed between text and icon in Persian times. The description of Anahita in the Avesta does, on the other hand, read like the description of a statue of Babylonian Ishtar. Two seal representations of Anahita show her, like Ishtar, standing on the back of a lion and receiving homage, whereas the Clercq cylinder shows her enthroned behind incense stands and wearing Urartian costume.

Fig. 54

Whilst we are no in a position to assess their precise relevance, these details of Persian religion are not out of place in considering the qualities of Persian character. Persian rule, if stern, was responsible and just. Injustice and unfairness were part of 'the Lie' whose advocates were destined to incur eternal punishment. Mithraism too had ethical teaching: Mithras was god of oaths and regulator of human conduct. With rectitude went bravery. Greek stories attest the bravery of Persian nobles, and Herodotus sums up the whole of Persian education as 'learning to ride and to shoot with a bow and to speak the truth'. The stress on hunting was not to foster sportsmanship, but to foster bravery and *truth,* since certain parts of the animal kingdom were part of 'the Lie'.

From the Zoroastrian religion of Achaemenid times many key concepts came into the Judaeo-Christian world and the universalism and idealism of the Persian empire, born of Zoroastrianism, can perhaps be claimed as more civilising in the long view than the ambitions of Periclean Athens. We must remember that much of our information about the Achaemenids comes from the pens of their traditional enemies. But Persia had admirers even among Greeks – Xenophon was one of them – and despite the despotism and cruelty, there is much witness to a 'high-mindedness' which was a key factor in the success of the empire.

THE ACHAEMENID FAMILY TO XERXES

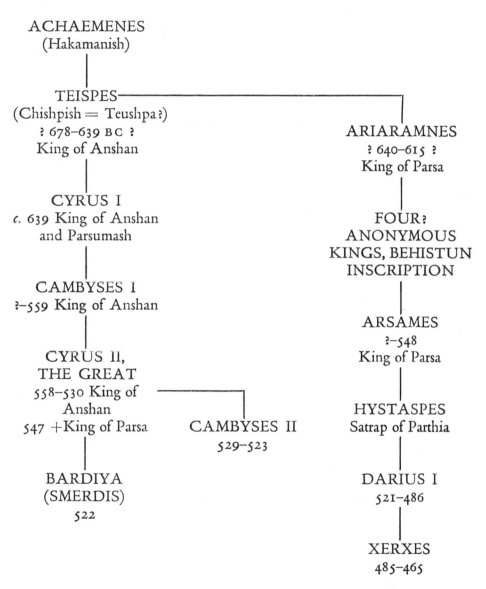

ACHAEMENES
(Hakamanish)

TEISPES
(Chishpish = Teushpa?)
? 678–639 BC ?
King of Anshan

ARIARAMNES
? 640–615 ?
King of Parsa

CYRUS I
c. 639 King of Anshan
and Parsumash

FOUR?
ANONYMOUS
KINGS, BEHISTUN
INSCRIPTION

CAMBYSES I
?–559 King of Anshan

ARSAMES
?–548
King of Parsa

CYRUS II,
THE GREAT
558–530 King of
Anshan
547 +King of Parsa

CAMBYSES II
529–523

HYSTASPES
Satrap of Parthia

BARDIYA
(SMERDIS)
522

DARIUS I
521–486

XERXES
485–465

Bibliography

Abbreviations

A.A.	*Artibus Asiae.*
A.J.A.	*American Journal of Archaeology.*
B.P.A.	*Bulletin of the American Institute of Persian Art and Archaeology.*
I.L.N.	*Illustrated London News.*
J.A.O.S.	*Journal of the American Oriental Society.*
J.H.S.	*Journal of Hellenic Studies.*
J.N.E.S.	*Journal of Near Eastern Studies.*
Pope, *Survey*	Pope, A. U. (ed.) *A Survey of Persian Art from Prehistoric Times to the Present,* vols. I and IV, London and New York, 1938.
S.A.	*Sovjetskaia Arkheologia.*

General Works of History and Culture

1   *Cambridge Ancient History,* vols III and IV, 1925–6.

2   CAMERON, G. G., *History of Early Iran,* Chicago, 1936.

3   GHIRSHMAN, R., *Iran,* London, 1954.

4   HERODOTUS, *The Histories.*

5, 6   HERZFELD, E., *Archaeological History of Iran,* Oxford, 1934; *Iran in the Ancient East,* Oxford, 1941.

7   OLMSTEAD, A. T., *History of the Persian Empire,* Chicago, 1948.

8   POPE, A. U. (ed.) *A Survey of Persian Art from Prehistoric Times to the Present,* vols I and IV, London and New York, 1938.

9   VANDEN BERGHE, G., *Archéologie de l'Iran ancien,* Leiden, 1959.

10   ZAEHNER, R. C., *The Dawn and Twilight of Zoroastrianism,* London, 1961.

Books and Articles of Detailed Studies

CHAPTER I *Metalsmiths and Migrants*

11 ACKERMAN, P., 'A Luristan Illustration of a Sunrise Ceremony', *The Cincinnati Art Museum Bull.*, V, 2, 1957, pp. 3–8.

12 ARNE, T. J., 'Luristan and the West', *Eurasia Septentrionalis Antiqua*, XI, 1934, p. 279 ff.

13 BUSCHOR, E., 'Eine Luristan-Kanne aus Samos', *Forschungen und Fortschritte*, XIII, 1932, p. 161.

14 CONTENAU, G., 'Les Bronzes du Luristan', *Genava*, XI, 1933, pp. 43–8.

15, 16 DEONNA, W., 'Bronzes du Luristan', *Genava*, X, 1932, pp. 84–98; *Les Musées de Genève*, IV, 10, 1947.

17 DESHAYES, J., 'Marteaux de Bronze iraniens', *Syria*, XXXV, 1958, pp. 284–93.

18 DUMEZIL, G., 'Dieux cassites et dieux védiques à propos d'un bronze du Luristan', *Revue hittite et asianique*, X, 1950, pp. 18–32.

19–21 DUSSAUD, R., 'The Bronzes of Luristan, Types and History', in Pope, *Survey*, pp. 254–77; 'Ceinture en bronze avec scènes de chasse', *Syria*, XV, 1934, pp. 185–99; 'Anciens bronzes du Louristan et cultes iraniens', *Syria*, XXVI, 1949, pp. 196–229.

22 DOSSIN, G., 'Bronzes inscrits du Luristan de la Collection Foroughi', *Iranica Antiqua*, II, (fasc. 2), 1962, pp. 151–64.

23 GHIRSHMAN, R., 'Notes iraniennes: Le dieu Zurvan sur les bronzes du Luristan', *A. A.*, XXI, 1958, pp. 37–42.

24 GODARD, A., 'Les bronzes du Luristan', *Ars asiatica*, 17, Paris, 1931.

25 HANCAR, F., 'Kaucasus-Luristan', *Eurasia Septentrionalis Antiqua*, IX, 1935, pp. 47–112.

26 KANTOR, H. J., 'Luristan Embossed Plaques', *J.N.E.S.*, 5, 1946, pp. 234–8.

27 LEGRAIN, L., *Luristan Bronzes in the University Museum*, Philadelphia, 1934.

28 MARYON, H., 'Early Near Eastern Steel Swords', *A.J.A.*, 65, 2, 1961, pp. 173–84.

29 NEEDLER, W. and SPENCE, M., 'An Iran Dagger from Luristan', *Bull. of the Royal Ontario Museum of Archaeology*, 23, 1955, pp. 14–24.

30 MOORTGAT, A., *Bronzegerät aus Luristan*, Berlin, 1932.

31 NAGEL, W., 'Die Königsdolche der zweiten Dynastie von Isin', *Archiv für Orientforschung*, XIX, 1961, pp. 95–104.

32 POPE, A. U., 'Dated Luristan Bronzes', *B.P.A.*, VII, 1934, pp. 19–20.

33, 34 POTRATZ, H. A., 'Die Luristanischen Pferdegebissen', *Prähistorische Zeitschrift* XXXII–XXXIII, 1941–2, pp. 169–234; 'Die Stangen Aufsätze in der Luristankunst', *Anadolu Arastirmalari* I, 1955, pp. 19–42.

35 SCHAEFFER, C. F. A., *Stratigraphie comparée et chronologie de l'Asie occidental*, Oxford, 1948, p. 477 ff.

36 SCHMIDT, E. F., 'The Second Holmes Expedition to Luristan', *B.P.A.*, V, 1937, pp. 205–16.

37 THIEME, P., 'The "Aryan" Gods of the Mitanni Treaties', *J.A.O.S.*, 80, 1960, pp. 301–17.

38 VAN WIJNGAARDEN, J., 'De Loeristanbronzen in het Rijksmuseum etc.', *Oudheidkundige Mededelinger van het Rijksmuseum van Oudheden te Leiden*, Supplement op Niewe Reeks XXXV, 1954.

CHAPTER II *Mannai, Medes and Scyths*

39 BARNETT, R. D., 'The treasure of Ziwiye', *Iraq*, XVIII, 1956, pp. 111–16.

40 CULICAN, W., 'The Hasanlu Bowl', *Milla-wa-Milla*, I, 1962, pp. 60–72.

41 DIAKONOV, M., *Istoria Medii*, Moscow–Leningrad, 1956 (in Russian).

42–46 DYSON, R. H., *University Museum Bull.*, Pennsylvania, XXII, 2, 1958, pp. 25–32; *Expedition*, I, 3, 1959, pp. 4–17 (with E. Porada), pp. 18–22; *Archaeology* XII, 1959, p. 134 ff.; *I.L.N.*, Jan 23, 1960, pp. 132–4; Feb 13, 1960, pp. 250–3.

47 FALKNER, M., 'Der Schatz von Ziwije', *Archiv für Orientforschung*, XVI, 1952–3, pp. 129–32.

48 GHIRSHMAN, R., 'Le trésor de Sakkez, les origines de l'art mède', *A.A.*, XIII, 1950, pp. 181–206.

49 GODARD, A., *Le trésor de Ziwiyé, (Kurdistan)*, Haarlem, 1950.

50, 51 KANTOR, H. J., 'A Bronze Deer from Iran', *Bull. of the Nelson Gallery and Atkins Museum*, 1962, pp. 3–8; 'A fragment of a gold appliqué from Ziwiye etc.', *J.N.E.S.*, XIX, 1960, pp. 3–17.

52 MALEKI, Y., 'Situle à scène de banquet', *Iranica Antiqua*, I, 1961, pp. 21–40.

53 MNATSAKANIAN, A. O., 'Excavations of Tumuli on the Shore of Lake Sevan in 1956', *S.A.*, 2, 1957, pp. 147–56.

54–56 NEGAHBAN, E. O., *I.L.N.*, April 28, 1962, 00. 663–4; May 5, 1962, pp. 699–701; 'A Brief Report on the Excavation of Marlik Tepe and Pileh Qal'eh', *Iran*, II, 1964.

57 PIOTROVSKY, B., *Vanskoye Tsarstvo*, Moscow, 1959.

58, 59 WILKINSON, C. K., 'More Details on Ziwiye', *Iraq*, XXII, 1960, pp. 213–20; 'Treasure from Mannean Land', *The Metropolitan Museum of Art Bull.*, April 1963, pp. 274–84.

CHAPTER III *Builders of Empire*

60 ATKINSON, K. M. T., 'The Legitimacy of Cambyses and Darius as Kings of Egypt', *J.A.O.S.*, 76, 3, 1956, pp. 167–85.

61 GADD, C., *The Fall of Nineveh*, London, 1923.

62 HERZFELD, E., 'Early Historical Contact between the Old Iranian

Empire and India', *India Antiqua, a Volume of Oriental Studies presented to J. P. Vogel,* Leiden, 1947, pp. 180–4.

63 KLASENS, A., 'Cambyses en Egypte', *Jaarbericht 'Ex Oriente Lux',* 10, 1945–8, pp. 339–49.

64 JUNGE, P., 'Saka Studien', *Klio Beiheft,* 24, Leipzig, 1939.

65 WEIDNER, E. F., 'Die älteste Nachricht über das persische Königshaus', *Archiv für Orientforschung,* VII, 1931, pp. 172–81.

CHAPTER IV *The Great Kings*

66 CAMERON, G. G., 'Darius' Daughter and the Persepolis Inscriptions', *J.N.E.S.,* I, 2, 1942, pp. 214–18.

67 CLAY, A. T., 'Gobryas, Governor of Babylonia, *J.A.O.S.,* 41, 1922.

68 HOW, W. W., 'Arms, Tactics and Strategy in the Persian War', *J.H.S.,* XLIII, 1932, pp. 117–32.

69 HOW, W. W., and WELLS, J., *A Commentary on Herodotus,* I–II, Oxford, 1949.

70–72 KENT, R. G., *Old Persian Grammar, Texts, Lexicon,* American Oriental Society, New Haven, Connecticut, 1950; 'Old Persian Texts: The Darius Suez C Inscription', *J.N.E.S.,* I, 4, 1942, pp. 415–23; 'The Naksh-i Rustam Inscriptions of Darius', *Language,* XV, 1939.

73 KING, L. W. and THOMPSON, R. C., '*The Sculptures and Inscriptions of Darius on the Rock of Behistun in Persia',* London, 1907.

74 OLMSTEAD, A. T., 'Darius and his Behistun Inscription', *American Journal of Semitic Languages,* 55, 1938, pp. 392–416.

75 POSENER, G., *La premier domination perse en Egypte: receuil d'inscriptions hieroglyphiques,* Cairo, 1963.

76 SMITH, S., *Babylonian Historical Texts Relating to the Capture and Downfall of Babylon,* London, 1924.

77 TARN, W. W., 'The Fleet of Xerxes', *J.H.S.,* XXVIII, 1908, pp. 202–33.

CHAPTER V *Palaces and Archives*

General

78 GHIRSHMAN, R., *Persia from the Origins to Alexander the Great*, London, 1964.

Architecture

79 AKURGAL, E., 'The Early Period and Golden Age of Ionia', *A.J.A.*, 66, 1962, pp. 369–79.

80 CASSON, S., 'The Aesthetic Character of Achaemenid Architecture', in Pope, *Survey*, 1938, pp. 330–5.

81 CONTENAU, G., 'Le prototype des chapiteaux achéménides', *Revue des arts asiatiques*, VII, 1931–2.

82 GHIRSHMAN, R., 'Masjid-i Solaiman', résidence des premiers Achéméni-des', *Syria*, XXVII, 1950, pp. 181–206.

83 HERZFELD, E., 'Bericht über die Ausgrabungen in Pasargadae', *Archäo-logische Mitteilungen aus Iran*, I, 1929, p. 16 ff.

84 LOSSEVA, E. M., 'Recent Archaeological Discoveries in Arin-berd', *S.A.*, 2, 1958, pp. 179–95 (in Russian).

85 MEQUENEM, R. de, 'Contribution a l'étude du palais achéménide de Suse', *Mémoires de la Mission archéologique en Iran*, XXX, Paris, 1947.

86 SCHMIDT, E. F., *Persepolis I: Structures, Reliefs, Inscriptions*, Chicago, 1953.

87 STRONACH, D., 'Excavations at Pasargadae, First Prelim. Report', *Iran*, I, 1963, pp. 19–42; 'Second Prelim. Report', *Iran* II, 1964, pp. 21–39.

Sculpture

88 BARNETT, R. D., 'Persepolis', *Iraq*, XIX, 1; 1957, pp. 53–77.

89 CASSON, S., 'Achaemenid Sculpture', in Pope, *Survey*, 1938, pp. 346–66.

90 ERDMANN, K., 'Griechische und Achämenidische Plastik', *Forschungen und Fortschritte*, XXVI, 11–12, 1950, pp. 150–3.

91 FRANKFORT, H., 'Achaemenian Sculpture', *A.J.A.*, 50, 1946, pp. 6–14.

92 GHIRSHMAN, R., 'Notes iraniennes VII: A propos de Persépolis', *A.A.*, XX, 1957, pp. 265–78.

93 RICHTER, G. M. A., 'The Greeks in Persia', *A.J.A.*, 50, 1946, p. 15–30.

94 ROES, A., 'The Achaemenid Robe', *Bibliotheca Orientalis*, VIII, 1951, pp. 137–41.

Inscriptions and Archives

95 CAMERON, G. G., *Persepolis Treasury Tablets*, Chicago, 1948.

96 DOUGHERTY, R. P., *Archives from Erech*, Goucher College Cuneiform Inscriptions, II, 1933.

97 MEQUENEM, R. de, and SCHEIL, V., *Inscriptions des Achéménides à Suse*, (Mémoires de la Mission archéologique de Perse XXI), Paris, 1929.

98 TREMAYNE, A., *Records from Erech, Time of Cyrus and Cambyses*, Yale U.P., 1925.

99 UNVALA, J. M., 'Achaemenid Architecture: Some Inscriptions', in Pope, *Survey*, 1938, pp. 336–45.

CHAPTER VI *Achaemenid Arts*

General

100 FRANKFORT, H., *Art and Architecture of the Ancient Orient*, 1959.

101 GOOSENS, G., 'Artistes et artisans étrangers en Perse sous les achéménides', *La Nouvelle Clio*, I, 1–2, 1949, pp. 32–44.

Seals

102 GADD, C. J., and ACKERMAN, P., 'Achaemenid Seals', in Pope, *Survey*, 1938, pp. 383–93.

103 NAGEL, W., 'Datierte Glyptik aus Altvorderasien', *Archiv für Orientforschung*, XX, 1963, pp. 125–40.

104 RICHTER, G. M. A., 'The Late Achaemenian or Greco-Persian Gems', *Hesperia*, suppl. VIII, 1949, pp. 291–8.

105 SEYRIG, H., 'Cachets achéménides', *Archaeologia Orientalia in Memoriam Ernst Herzfeld,* New York, 1952, pp. 195–202.

106 STRELKOFF, A., 'The Moscow Cylinder Seals', *B.P.A.,* V, 1937, p. 17 ff.

Toreutics, Stone Vessels and Glass

107-109 AMANDRY, P., 'Toreutique achéménide', *Antike Kunst* II, 1959, pp. 38–48; 'Newly Found Achaemenian Gold and Silver', *I.L.N.,* Dec. 27th, 1958, pp. 1140–2; May 23rd, 1959, pp. 892–3.

110 CINCINNATI ART MUSEUM, *Bulletin,* VI, 1–4, July 1961. Rock crystal bowl no. 1957–500.

111 CORNING MUSEUM OF GLASS, *Glass from the Ancient World,* Exhibition Catalogue, 1960.

112 FOSSING, P., 'Drinking Bowls of Glass and Metal from the Achaemenian Time', *Berytus,* IV, 1937, pp. 121–9.

113 GHIRSHMAN, R., 'Notes iraniennes: Un plat achéménide de la coll. Foroughi', *A.A.,* XXIV, 1961, pp. 39–44.

114 HAAGSGEMEENTE MUSEUM, *7000 jaar Perzische Kunst,* Exhibition Catalogue, The Hague, 1962.

115 KUNSTHAUS ZÜRICH, *Kunstschätze aus Iran,* Exhibition Catalogue, Neue Zürcher Zeitung, 1962 (a closely similar version is the catalogue *7000 Jahre Kunst in Iran,* Villa Hügel, Essen, 1964).

116 HOFFMAN, H., 'The Persian Origin of Attic Rhyta', *Antike Kunst,* IV, 1961, pp. 21–6.

117 SCHMIDT, E. F., *Persepolis II; Contents of the Treasury and Other Discoveries,* Chicago, 1957.

118 SMIRNOV, J. I., *Oriental Silver,* Leningrad, 1909 (in Russian).

119 SVOBODA, B., and CONČEV, D., *Neue Denkmäler Antiker Toreutik,* Prague, 1956.

120 TERRACE, E. L. B., 'Two Achaemenian Objects in the Boston Museum of Fine Arts', *Antike Kunst,* VI, 2, 1963, pp. 72–80.

121 WILKINSON, C. K., 'Assyrian and Persian Art', *The Metropolitan Museum of Art Bull.,* XIII, March 1955, pp. 213–24.

122 WOOLLEY, C. L., 'A Drinking Horn from Asia Minor', *Annals of Archaeology and Anthropology,* X, Liverpool, 1923, pp. 69–72.

Jewellery

123 AMANDRY, P., Orfèvrerie achéménide', *Antike Kunst,* I, 1958, pp. 9–23.

124 DALTON, O. M. *The Treasure of the Oxus,* British Museum, London, 1926, repr. 1964.

125 FRANKFORT, H., 'A Persian Goldsmith's Trial Piece', in *J.N.E.S.,* IX, 1950, pp. 111–12.

126 KANTOR, H. J., 'Achaemenid Jewellery in the Oriental Institute', *J.N.E.S.,* XVI, 1957, p. 9–20.

127 MORGAN, J. de, 'Découverte d'une sépulture achéménide à Suse', *Mémoires de la Délégation en Perse,* VIII, Paris, 1905.

128 RICE, D. TALBOT, 'Achaemenid Jewellery', in Pope, *Survey,* 1938, pp. 377–82.

Metalwork and Armour

129 BOYSAL, Y., 'Urartian Work etc. at Aznavur', *Turk Tarih Kurumu Belleten,* XXV, 98, 1961, pp. 199–209 (in Turkish).

130 GOLDMAN, B., 'Achaemenian Chapes', *Ars Orientalis,* 2, 1957, pp. 43–54.

131 HALL, H. R., 'Bronze Forepart of an Ibex', *The Antiquaries Journal,* 9, 1929, pp. 217–18.

132 PARROT, A., 'Acquisitions et inédits du Musée du Louvre', *Syria,* XXX, 1953, pp. 1–11.

133 RUEPPEL, M. C., 'Bronze Sculpture from Ancient Persia', *Bull. Minneapolis Institute of Arts,* 1957.

134 SHEPHERD, D. G., 'A Bronze Sculpture from Iran', *Bull. Cleveland Museum of Art,* XLVIII, 10, 1961, pp. 254–8.

135 THOMPSON, D. B., 'The Persian Spoils in Athens', *The Aegean and Near*

East: *Essays presented to H. Goldman,* ed. S. Weinberg, New York, 1956, pp. 281–91.

136 WILKINSON, C. K., 'An Achaemenian Bronze Head', *The Metropolitan Museum of Art Bull.,* Nov. 1956, pp. 72–8.

CHAPTER VII *From the Satrapies*

General

137 AZARPAY, G., 'Some Classical and Near Eastern Motifs in the Art of Pasyryk', *A.A.,* XXII, 1959, pp. 313–39.

138 ROES, A., 'Achaemenid Influence on Egyptian and Nomad Art', *A.A.,* XV, 1952, pp. 17–30.

Iraq and Iran

139 BASMACHI, F., 'Nippur', *Sumer,* IX, 2, 1953, pp. 281–95.

140 GHIRSHMAN, R., *Village Perse-Achéménide,* Mémoires de la Mission archéologique en Iran, XXXVI, Paris, 1954.

141 QADIR AL-TAKRIT, A., 'Excavations at Tell Deim', *Sumer,* XVI, 1 and 2, 1960, pp. 93–111.

142 ROBINSON, E. S. G., 'A Silversmith's Hoard from Mesopotamia', *Iraq,* XIII, 1950, pp. 44–51.

143 WOOLLEY, Sir L., *Ur Excavations,* vol. IX, London, 1962, pp. 249–66.

Asia Minor

144 AKURGAL, E., 'Les fouilles de Daskyleion', *Anatolia,* I, 1956, p. 20 ff.

145 BALKAN, K., 'Inscribed Bullae from Daskyleion-Ergili', *Anatolia,* IV, 1959, pp. 123–8.

146 YOUNG, R., 'The Campaign of 1955 at Gordion: Preliminary Report', *A.J.A.,* 60, 1956, pp. 249–66; 'The 1961 Campaign at Gordion', *A.J.A.,* 66, 1962, pp. 155–68.

Syria

148, 149 CARRIÈRE, B. and BARROIS, A., 'Fouilles de l'ecole francaise de

Jérusalem', (Neirab), *Syria,* VIII, 2, 1927, pp. 126–42; 3, pp. 201–5; IX, 3, 1928, pp. 185–206; 4, pp. 301–18.

150 WOOLLEY, C. L., 'A North Syrian Cemetery of the Persian Period', *Annals of Anthropology and Archaeology,* VII, 3–4, Liverpool, 1916, pp. 115–29.

Palestine

151 LAPP, P. W., 'Late Royal Seals from Judah', *Bull. of the American School of Oriental Research,* no. 158, 1960 pp. 11–22.

152 ILIFFE J. H., 'A Tell Fara Tomb Group Reconsidered', *Quarterly of the Department of Antiquities of Palestine,* IV, 4, pp. 182–6.

153 MACALISTER, R. A. S., *The Excavation of Gezer,* London, 1912.

154 PETRIE, W. M. F., *Beth Pelet,* I, London, 1930.

South Russia

155 BARNETT, R. D., 'Median Art', *Iranica Antiqua,* II, 1962, pp. 77–95.

156 HANČAR, F., 'The Eurasian Animal Style and the Altai complex', *A.A.,* XV, 1952, pp. 171–94.

157 HARIMANOV, E. G., 'Sar Tepe', *S.A.,* 1957, 3 (in Russian)

158 MANTSEVITCH, A. P., 'An ox-head from a sixth century Tumulus at Kalitva', *S.A.,* 1958, 2, pp. 196–202 (in Russian).

159 ROSTOVTZEFF, M., *Iranians and Greeks in South Russia,* Oxford, 1922.

160 RUDENKO, C. E., *The Popular Culture of the Central Altai in the Scythian Period,* Moscow–Leningrad, 1960 (in Russian).

161 SMIRNOV, J. I., *Der Schatzfund Achalgori,* Tiflis, 1934.

Bulgaria

162 FILOW, B., *Die Grabhügelnekropole bei Duvanlij,* Sofia, 1934.

163 CONČEV, D., *Der Goldschatz von Panagjurishte,* Prague, 1956.

Egypt

164, 165 COONEY, J. D., 'The Portrait of an Egyptian Collaborator'; 'The

Lions of Leontopolis', *Bull. of the Brooklyn Museum,* XV, 2, 1953, pp. 1–30.

166 LEFEBRE, G., *Le Tombeau de Petosiris,* Paris, 1924.

167 POSENER, G., *La prémière domination perse en Egypte: Recueil d'inscriptions hieroglyphiques,* Cairo, 1936.

168, 169 RABINOWITZ, I., 'Aramaic Inscriptions of the Fifth Century BC', *J.N.E.S.,* XV, 1956, 1, pp. 1–9; 'Another Aramaic Record of the North Arabian Goddess Han-'Ilat', *J.N.E.S.,* XVIII, 1959, 2, pp. 154–5.

CHAPTER VIII *The Later History*

170 BRESCIANI, E., 'Papiri aramaici egiziani etc. presso il Museo Civico di Padova', *Rivista degli studi orientali,* XXXV, 1960.

171 BRIGHT, J., *A History of Israel,* London, 1960.

172 BURN, A. R., *Persia and the Greeks,* London, 1962.

173 CROSS, F. M., 'The Discovery of the Samaria Papyri', *Biblical Archaeologist,* XXVI, 4, 1963, pp. 110–21.

174 DRIVER, G. R., *Aramaic Documents of the Fifth Century BC,* Oxford, 1954.

175 KRAELING, K., *The Brooklyn Museum Aramaic Papyri,* New Haven, 1953.

176 XENOPHON, *The Persian Expedition,* trans. Rex Warner, London, 1949.

CHAPTER IX *The Pulse of Power*

177 HILL, G. F., *Greek Coins of Arabia, Mesopotamia and Persia,* London. 1922.

178 HINZ, W., *Zarathustra,* Stuttgart, 1961.

179 MULLER, M., (ed.), *The Zend Avesta* (Sacred Books of the East, XXIII), Oxford, 1883.

180 NYBERG, N. S., *Die Religionen des Alten Iran,* Leipzig, 1938.

181 POSTAN, M. M., 'The Rise of a Money Economy', *Economic History Review,* XIV, 1944, pp. 123–34.

182   STROUVE, V. V., 'The Religion of the Achaemenids and Zoroastrianism *Cahiers d'histoire mondiale,* 5, 1959–60, pp. 529–45.

183   EGGERMONT, P. H. L., Indië en de Hellenisticshe Rijken', *Jaarbericht 'Ex Oriente Lux',* 8, 1942, pp. 736–46.

184   ROWLAND, B., 'Hellenistic Sculpture in Iran', *The Art Quarterly,* XVIII, 2, 1955, pp. 174–9.

Note

Among recent treatments of controversial matters covered by this book may be noted R. Ghirshman's 'A propos des bronzes du Luristan de la collection Foroughi', *Iranica Antigua,* II, 2, 1962, in which he states his views on the origin of early inscribed bronzes. For a different analysis of bronzework see E. Porada, *Iran Ancien,* Paris, 1963. The circumstances of Darius' accession are discussed by R. N. Frye in *The Heritage of Persia,* London, 1962, p. 88 ff., which should be read in conjunction with A. Poebel, 'The Reign of Smerdis and Others', *American Journal of Semitic Languages,* 56 (1959), pp. 121–45.

THE PLATES

1   2

3

4

5

6

7

8

9

10

11

12

13

14

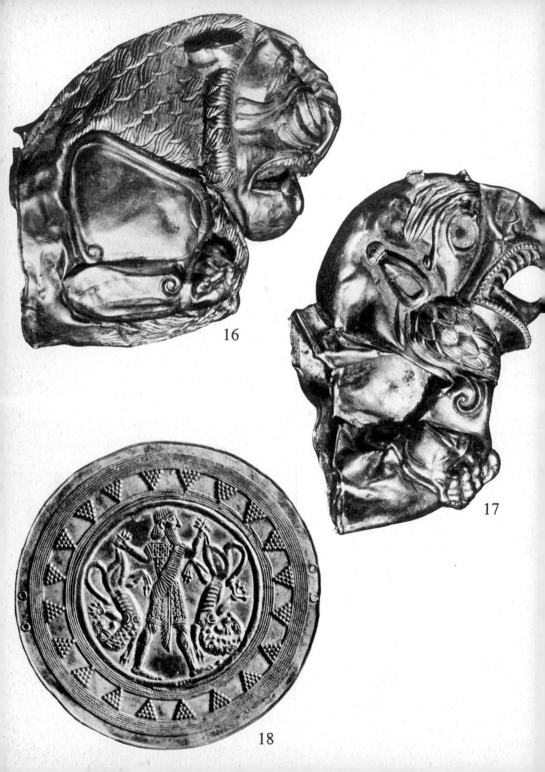

16

17

18

19

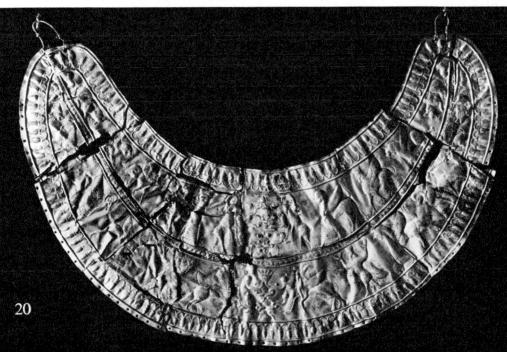

20

21

23

24

26

27

28

29

30

31

32

33

34

38

39

41

42

44

45

46

47   48

49

50

51

52

53

54

55

56

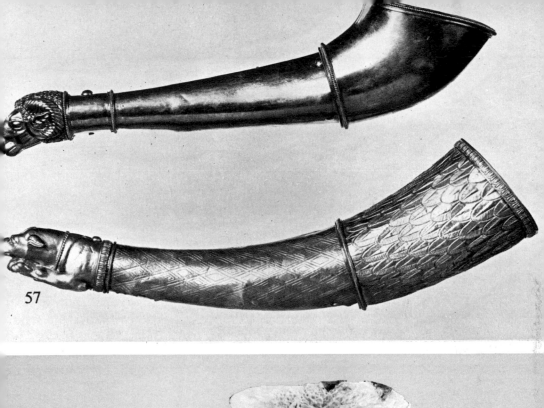

57

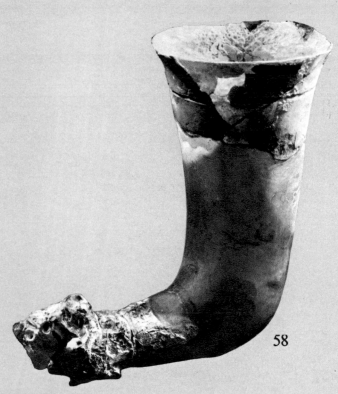

58

59

60

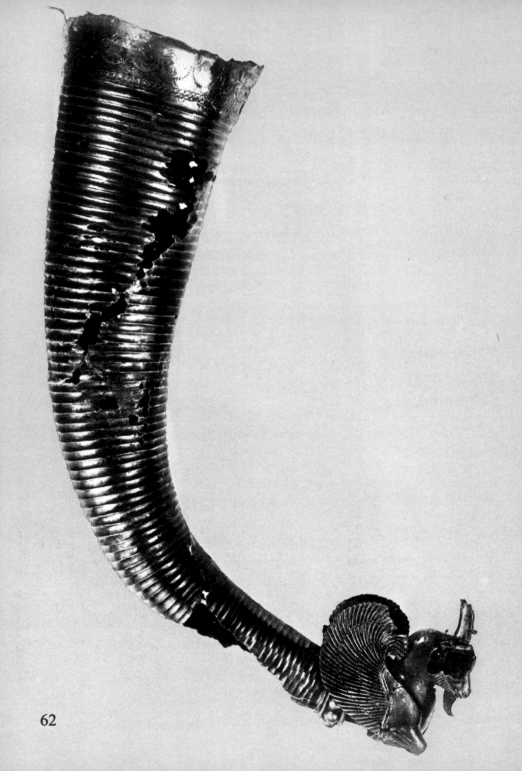

63

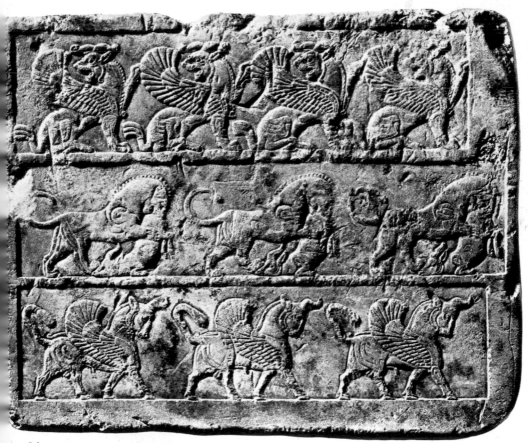

64

67

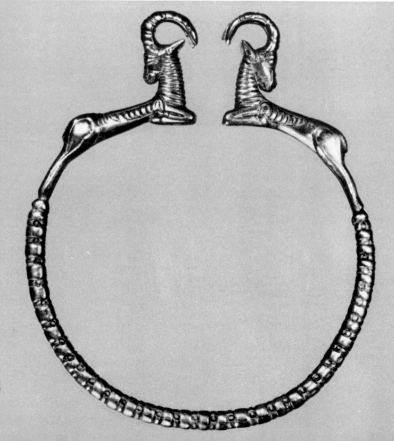

68

69

70

72

73

74

Notes on the Plates

The bracketed figures on the end of each note refer to the work in the Select Bibliography, in which each object is published or in which related material is discussed.

1, 2 Bronze drinking cup or situla from Luristan, embossed with a banquet scene in which a seated nobleman is attended by his cup-bearer and musician. Other items are wine vessels with syphons and an Assyrian 'Fountain vase' topped with palms. Ht 6½ in. Eighth-seventh century B C. Metropolitan Museum, New York (Rogers Fund). (8, 30, 52)

3 Bronze ritual bucket from Luristan, the body embossed with goats and flowers of Assyrian style, the handle cast in the indigenous Luristan fashion. Ht 8⅔ in. Eighth century B C. Cincinnati Art Museum. (11)

4 Silver strip, Luristan. The central figure is possibly the god Zurvan, the Indo-Aryan god of time, surrounded by figures in 'three ages of man' – childhood, virility, old age. 4⅝ × 10⅛ in. Eighth century B C. Cincinnati Art Museum. (23)

5 Embossed disc-head of a Luristan bronze votive pin from Surkh Dum. The central lion-head boss is a symbol of the sun. The tall winged central figure appears to be a vegetation deity feeding wild goats. The dragons on his shoulders are borrowed from Akkadian art and symbolise power. The whole concept is, however, a cosmic one, as shown by the radiant stars on the circumference. Diam. 4 in. Eighth century B C. University Museum, Philadelphia. (21)

6 Gold bowl from Hasanlu near Lake Urmia. The repoussé scenes are enhanced by a refined engraving. A procession of weather gods in chariots makes up the upper frieze; below, a series of isolated scenes appears to belong to a cycle of myths of Hurrian origin, although some of the motifs appear to be Akkadian. The base is engraved with a formal

design of sheep walking on the four sides of a chequer-board. Ht 8½ in., diam. 11 in. Teheran Archaeological Museum. (Photo Bulloz) (41, 43)

7, 8 Electrum beaker from north-west Iran, related in technique to the Hasanlu bowl, in shape to the Amlash and Marlik Tepe beakers. A motif of a double-headed lion-bodied monster with human arms and the wings and talons of an eagle, lifting mountain goats by the tail, is repeated three times. On the base is a circular pattern of fishes. Ht 4½ in. Ninth-eighth centuries BC. Louvre, Paris. A. Parrot, 'Acquisitions et inédits du Musée du Louvre', *Syria*, XXXV, 1958.

9–12 Pottery of interesting shapes from Amlash and Daylaman in north-west Iran. The bird-like jugs (10, 11) with women's faces are 5–6 inches high and were perhaps children's feeders. The bottle in the form of a female figure (12) is over 17 inches high and is one of a considerable group of such vessels. The face-spouted bull-jug (9) is also now represented by numerous examples ranging from 8 to 14 inches in length. The pottery has a bright tile-red polished surface decorated with incised circles and occasional spots of black paint. Tenth-ninth centuries BC. Museum of Fine Arts, Boston. (54–56) Cf. R. Ghirshman, 'Notes iraniennes XI: Le rhyton en Iran', *Artibus Asiae*, XXV, 1963.

13 Group of miniature bronze animals from Daylaman in north-west Iran, including a stag, humped bull, horse and rider and dog. The horse was little used as a mount in western Asia and cavalry was probably intro-duced by the northern nomads. These miniatures, intended both for standing and suspension, are known also from Amlash and Marlik Tepe as well as from Talish and Armenia. Ninth century BC. Museum of fine Arts, Boston. (50)

14 Gold beaker from Amlash with three rows of sphinxes in mixed Assyrian and Luristan style. Ht 4¾ in. Eighth century BC. Teheran Archaeological Museum. (Photo Bulloz) (114, 115)

15 Bronze stag from north-west Iran. Related pieces come from Soviet Armenia and Lenkoran. Ht 10 in. Nelson Gallery – Atkins Museum (Nelson Fund), Kansas City, Missouri. (50)

16, 17   Two of two pairs of griffin and lion mounts of beaten gold from the Ziwiyeh treasure. The griffin is closely related to Urartian griffin heads, which are themselves ancestral to the *protomai* or archaic Greek ritual cauldrons. Lion *protomai* are also found on Greek cauldrons and it has been assumed that these pieces also were attached to vessels or furniture. Ht about $3\frac{1}{4}$ in. Seventh century BC. Teheran Archaeological Museum. (Photo J. Powell) (48, 49)

18   One of a number of roundels found at Khafantlu (ancient Izirtu?) near Ziwiyeh, depicting the god-hero Gilgamesh lifting lions. Border of soldered wire strands and triangles of granules. Diam. $2\frac{3}{4}$ in. Seventh century BC. Nelson Gallery – Atkins Museum (Nelson Fund), Kansas City, Missouri. *The Nelson Gallery and Atkins Museum Bulletin*, Spring 1961.

19   Penannular gold arm-ring from Ziwiyeh. One of the pair of lion-head terminals can be removed and refastened with a pin. The middle broadens into two flat triangular flanges decorated with antithetical pairs of lion cubs. Greatest diam. $3\frac{7}{12}$ in. Seventh century BC. Teheran Archaeological Museum. (Photo J. Powell) (49, 59)

20   Crescentic gold pectoral from the Ziwiyeh treasure decorated with a procession of mythical animals facing inwards towards sacred trees. Note the crouched Scythian animals (bear and hare) in the extremities. Length $13\frac{1}{4}$ in. Late seventh century BC. Teheran Archaeological Museum. (Photo J. Powell) (47, 49, 51)

21   Ivory plaque of Assyrian workmanship, Ziwiyeh treasure. Ht $5\frac{7}{8}$ in. Seventh century BC. Teheran Archaeological Museum. (Photo J. Powell) (39, 58) Cf. C. K. Wilkinson, 'Some New Contacts with Nimrud and Assyria', *The Metropolitan Museum of Art Bulletin*, X, 8, 1952.

22   Embossed and engraved gold plaque with scenes of an Assyrian warrior in close combat with a lion, from Ziwiyeh. $4\frac{3}{4} \times 2\frac{7}{8}$ in. Seventh century BC. Teheran Archaeological Museum. (Photo J. Powell) (49, 58, 59)

23 Carved ivory with an Assyrian-derived theme, of local Mannaean workmanship, from the Ziwiyeh treasure. The dress of the figures is found in Luristan art. Length $5\frac{7}{8}$ in. Seventh century BC. Teheran Archaeological Museum. (Photo J. Powell) (49)

24 Gold plaque from Ziwiyeh, with winged lions rearing against a sacred tree. The style of the lions prefigures that of Achaemenid lions and the style of the sacred tree resembles that on certain Amlash pieces. It is probably Median. Ht $4\frac{1}{8}$ in. Seventh century BC. H. Kevorkian Collection, New York. (Photo Giraudon) (114, 115)

25 Detail of a silver plate with gold appliqué animal figures of Scythian style, from the Ziwiyeh region. The leaf-like motifs of the inner circle are derivations of Assyrian lotus buds. The bowl bears an inscription in undeciphered pictographic script. Diam. $14\frac{3}{4}$ in. Late seventh century BC. Teheran Archaeological Museum. (Photo J. Powell) (48, 49)

26 Median gold cup with two handles in the form of stylized rearing lions, found in Luristan. On the body, a pair of lions share the same head in relief. Ht $5\frac{5}{12}$ in. Seventh–sixth centuries BC. H. Kevorkian Collection. (Photo Giraudon) (114)

27 Gold cup with handles in the form of double-headed ibexes, so far unique and probably Median. The flutings on the body are sharply delineated as on other vessels from Hamadan, where this piece is said to have been found. The lions are similar to certain lions on Ziwiyeh plaques (cf. Plate 24) whilst the frieze of open palms and buds on the base is an Assyrian motif popular on Luristan beaten bronzes. Ht $4\frac{3}{8}$ in. Seventh century BC. Cincinnati Art Museum. (11, 51)

28 Silver amphora with bull-handles. Both the lotus frieze and the Assyrian or Urartian styling of the bulls indicate an early, possibly seventh-century date. Ht. $6\frac{1}{3}$ in. Private Collection, Geneva. (Photo Giraudon) (114)

29 Small bronze goblet terminating in a lion's head, from north-west Iran. The lower jaw forms a handle. Median or possibly Urartian. Eighth

century B C. Pomerance Collection, New York. (Photo Giraudon) R. Ghirshman, 'Notes iraniennes XI: Le rhyton en Iran', *Artibus Asiae*, XXV, 1963.

30 Small attachment, perhaps for a shield, of a silver ram's head with sleeve bound with twisted wire and decorated with pyramids of granules. It comes from Khafantlu near Ziwiyeh and the granulation and wire is similar to that of the Khafantlu plaque (Plate 18). Length 3 in. Seventh century B C. Nelson Gallery – Atkins Museum (Nelson Fund), Kansas City, Missouri. *The Nelson Gallery and Atkins Museum Bulletin,* Spring 1961.

31 Whetstone handle in the form of a gazelle head; gold with raised dot-work imitating granulation. Note the petal-shaped matrix for inlay on the head and the elongated ears. It is typical of the group of whetstone handles from Hamadan. Length about 3 in. Sixth century B C. Teheran Archaeological Museum. (Photo Giraudon) (114, 115)

32 Rhyton from Marash in south-east Turkey, the base in the form of a kneeling golden bull, the horn of silver and undecorated. The feather-like stylisation of the hair on the head and chest of the bull, as well as the thick neck, suggest Urartian affinities. Probably Median work. Ht $7\frac{3}{4}$ in. Seventh century B C. British Museum. (122)

33 Golden rhyton from Hamadan (ancient Ecbatana), the body in the form of a snarling winged lion; the lip of the horn is decorated with a formal frieze of alternate lotus buds and blooms. This is one of the most dynamic pieces of Achaemenid art and despite the formal rendering and stylis-ation incorporates a piece of genuine natural observation in the folded ear of the lion on close guard. Ht $8\frac{3}{4}$ in. Sixth century B C. Teheran Archaeological Museum. (Photo J. Powell) (114, 115, 121)

34 Necklace of granulated gold and turquoise beads with ten openwork pendants each with a pair of lions crossed. These pendants are similar to openwork pieces designed as costume jewellery. Length about 17 in. Sixth century B C. Teheran Archaeological Museum. (Photo J. Powell) (123, 126)

35 Golden short sword from Hamadan (Ecbatana) with hilt and blade in one piece. The hilt terminates with addorsed lions' heads the fine work and style of which is exactly paralleled in bracelet terminals. Note the oblique strands of stiff hair beneath the ears, typical of Hamadan lions. The juncture of hilt and blade is ornamented by two bearded ibex heads. A somewhat similar dagger hilt is in the Metropolitan Museum, New York. Length 17¾ in. Sixth century BC. Teheran Archaeological Museum. (Photo J. Powell) (114, 115, 121)

36 Gold plaque with cut-out inscription of Darius from the foundations of the Apadana at Persepolis. There are ten lines of Persian, seven of Babylonian, eight of Elamite – all extolling Ahuramazda and stating the extent of the Empire from Lydia to India. Similar gold foundation plaques of Arsames, Darius and Artaxerxes II have been found at Hamadan. 12¾ × 13 in. Late sixth century BC. Teheran Archaeological Museum. (Photo Dräyer) (9, 70, 114, 115)

37 View of the ruins of Persepolis from east to west. In the foreground is the Hall of a Hundred Columns with many of the column bases still in position. In the centre of the picture are the three doorways of the Tripylon. In the background, overlooking the Plain of Assembly is the Palace of Darius. In the right centre of the picture a modern protective building covers the sculptured staircase of the Tripylon. (Photo Perissinotto) (86)

38 North Syrian or Anatolian tribute-bearers bringing as gifts drinking bowls and a pair of armlets terminating in winged griffins. From the north side of the eastern stairway of Darius' apadana, completed under Xerxes. Persepolis. (Photo Perissinotto) (86, 88)

39 Scythian tribute-bearer carrying a spout-handled amphora passing one of Darius' conifers. Relief from the eastern apadana stairway at Persepolis. (Photo Perissinotto) (86, 108)

40 Relief of Darius entering the Tripylon or Central Hall at Persepolis. One of his attendants carries the parasol, the other the fly-whisk and towel. (Photo Perissinotto) (86, 92)

41   Part of the relief on the Tripylon stair at Persepolis: Median nobles in procession to the banquet hall carrying lilies. In order to keep the heads on the same level the sculptor has interposed giant and dwarf figures. (Photo Perissinotto) (86, 92)

42   Persepolis: relief on the inner balustrade: The Persian nobility mounting the stairs into the Tripylon or Central Hall. Note the torque worn by the first figure in the group. Persepolis. (Photo Perissinotto) (86, 92)

43   'Fire-temple' at Naqsh-i Rustam which stands in front of the tomb of Darius I (Plate 76). It is built of dressed limestone blocks with three rows of recessed 'blind windows' of black stone. The entrance was level with the second tier of windows and reached by a flight of stairs giving access to a single room. The roofing has not survived and its use as a fire shrine is conjectural. A similar tower was built at Pasargadae. Ht 32 ft, width 23 ft. Sixth to fifth centuries BC. (Photo Perissinotto) (86, 88, 178)

44   Gold gadrooned bowl inscribed in Persian with the name of Darius, probably Darius I, from Hamadan. Ht $4\frac{1}{2}$ in., diam. $7\frac{3}{4}$ in. Sixth-fifth centuries BC. Metropolitan Museum, New York (Dick Fund 1954). (121)

45   Gold gadrooned drinking cup from Hamadan (Ecbatana) with trilingual inscription in the name of Xerxes, who established his royal treasury at Ecbatana. Ht $4\frac{7}{10}$ in., diam. $8\frac{1}{8}$ in. Fifth century BC. Teheran Archaeological Museum. (Photo J. Powell) (114)

46   Remarkably preserved rock crystal bowl of Late Assyrian or possibly early Achaemenid workmanship. A lioness attacks a herd of fleeing bulls, engaging one of them in a combat scene of a type generally favoured by Achaemenid artists. Diam. $5\frac{3}{8}$ in. Seventh–sixth centuries BC. Cincinnati Art Museum. (110)

47, 48   Two views of a grey schist statue of an Egyptian official Ptah-hotep, wearing a Persian jacket and an ibex-ended torque. The hieroglyphic inscription on a panel on the back names him as minister of finance and of all royal works. Ht $32\frac{1}{2}$ in. XXVII Dynasty. Brooklyn Museum (Wilbour Collection). (164)

49 Gold cup in the form of a ram's head with granulation on the rim Ht 4⅛ in. Sixth-fifth centuries BC. Metropolitan Museum, New York. *The Metropolitan Museum of Art Bulletin*, XVI, 2, 1957.

50 Deep drinking bowl of silver, the body covered with an open water-lily with feathery stamens. Ht 4¾ in. Fourth century BC. Brooklyn Museum. J. D. Cooney, *Five Years of Collecting Egyptian Art*, Brooklyn Museum, 1956.

51 A bronze amphora, probably Median, found in Syria. The dissimilar handles are in the forms of a bull and a goat, with the back of the bull-handle forming a tubular spout. Ht 7½in. *c.* 630 BC. Burrell Collection, Glasgow Museum and Art Gallery. (108)

52 Carved slab showing the funeral rites of a Persian official, found at Memphis, in Egypt. The mourners include trousered Scythian servants and the deceased's groom and horse, women-servants baring their breasts and tearing their hair (traditional signs of Egyptian mourning) and a pair of sirens. The furniture is Persian. Width 18 in. Sixth century BC. Formerly Berlin Museum. Freiherr von Bissing, *Zeitschrift der Deutschen Morgenländischen Gesellschaft*, 84, 1930.

53 Shallow gold dish with a flying bird as centrepiece, from Hamadan. Similar birds are known on Ziwiyeh pieces and spread to Scythian art. Diam. 12¾ in. Sixth-fifth centuries BC. H. Kevorkian Collection, New York. (Photo Giraudon) (114, 115)

54 Shallow silver dish found at Sinope on the Black Sea coast. The lotus flowers and the central medallion are gilded. Diam. 7⅗ in. Fifth century BC. Museum of Fine Arts, Boston. (120)

55 Silver rhyton from the Seven Brothers Tombs in the south Russian Koban, first half fifth century BC. Hermitage Museum, Leningrad. (118, 119)

56 Silver rhyton in the shape of a kneeling bull. The bull wears a collar like that on the Persepolis bull-capitals. The folds of flesh about the mouth

and the high position of the nostrils are unusual. Ht 9¼ in. Sixth‑fifth centuries B C. Cincinnati Art Museum. (107)

57   Pair of gold horn‑rhyta from Tomb 4, Seven Brothers Tombs, south Russian Koban, with terminals in the form of a ram's head and a dog's head showing Greek influence, fifth‑fourth centuries B C. Hermitage Museum, Leningrad. (118, 119)

58   Rhyton of grey‑green glass. The base ends in the forepart of a bull with a lion attacking its neck. Parts of the bull are inlaid with blue plaste. The centre part of the horn is restored. Teheran Archaeological Museum. (Photo Dräyer) (113)

59   Goblet of dark‑green glass, probably Achaemenid. It belongs to a small group of early glass vessels made by cutting and lathe‑turning as in working rock crystal and alabaster. A similarly made vessel inscribed with the name of King Sargon was found at Nimrud and it is probable that the Achaemenids continued this Assyrian technique, besides pro‑ ducing cut glass paterae. Ht 7$\frac{11}{16}$ in. Seventh‑fifth centuries B C. The Corning Museum of Glass, New York. (111) Cf. A. von Saldern, 'Achaemenid and Sassanian Cut Glass', *Ars Orientalis*, V, 1963.

60   Stone bowl in the shape of a crouching mountain goat, a beautifully delineated piece despite the mistaken carving of the back legs. Length 14¾ in. Sixth‑fifth centuries B C. Brooklyn Museum (Guennol Collec‑ tion, courtesy Mr and Mrs Alastair Bradley Martin).

61   Large vessel of carved stone supported on the backs of three ibexes, the bodies of which join beneath the bowl. Closely related to metalwork. Ht 24 in. Sixth‑fifth centuries B C. Private Collection, Geneva. (Photo Giraudon) (109, 114, 115)

62   Silver horn‑rhyton from Tomb 4 of the Seven Brothers Tombs, south Russian Koban, first half fifth century B C. Hermitage Museum, Lenin‑ grad. (118, 119)

63 A curious limestone amulet (?) carved with addorsed lions' and rams' heads, possibly from Egypt. Length 3½in. Sixth century BC. Brooklyn Museum. (164)

64 Carved limestone plaque, probably a goldsmith's die-piece, found in Egypt. $9\frac{11}{21} \times 8\frac{2}{3}$ in. Fifth century BC. By courtesy of the Oriental Institute, University of Chicago. (125)

65 Bronze ibex head, hollow-cast, probably a fitment for a piece of furniture. A number of similar pieces are known. Ht $6\frac{3}{4}$ in. Sixth-fifth centuries BC. Cleveland Museum of Art (Gift of Katherine Holden Thayer). (134)

66 Bronze sculpture of a Persian nobleman, Hamadan. Ht. $9\frac{3}{4}$ in. Similar figures were found with the Oxus treasure. Fifth century BC. Institute of Arts, Minneapolis. (78)

67 Crescentic earring of Achaemenid style with a central figure of the Egyptian god Bes. Diam. $1\frac{1}{2}$ in. Fifth century BC. Louvre Museum, Paris. E. Coche de la Ferté, *Les bijoux antiques*, Paris, 1956.

68 Gold bracelet. Diam. $3\frac{3}{5}$ in. Sixth-fifth centuries BC. Courtesy of the City Art Museum, St Louis, Missouri. (123)

69 Costume ornament; gold bracteate with two rampant lions. Diam. $1\frac{5}{8}$ in. Hamadan. Fifth century BC. Seattle Art Museum (Eugene Fuller Memorial Collection). (126)

70 Costume ornament; gold horned-griffin head. Width $1\frac{7}{16}$ in. Hamadan. Fifth century BC. Seattle Art Museum (Eugene Fuller Memorial Collection). (126)

71 One of a pair of amphora handles in the form of a winged ibex, silver with gilded wings and other features. The lower handle attachment, formed of a Silenus head with palmette, shows Greek influence. Found in Armenia. The other handle of the pair is in the Louvre. Ht $10\frac{7}{2}$ in.

About 380 BC. Antikenabteilung der Staatlichen Museen, West Berlin. (8, 107)

72 A silver mountain sheep with gold face and beard, found in India. Length 2½in. Fifth century BC. Museum of Fine Arts, Boston. (120)

73 Silver model antelope intended for suspension. Length 4 in. Fourth century BC. Metropolitan Museum, New York. C. K. Wilkinson, 'The Art of the Ancient Near East', *The Metropolitan Museum of Art Bulletin*, VII, 7, 1949.

74 Sculptured head from Hamadan (Ecbatana), possibly the head of a winged bull. Ht 19¾ in. Fifth century BC. Nelson Gallery – Atkins Museum, Kansas, Missouri (Nelson Fund).

75 Miniature jewel-like head of sculptured lapis lazuli. Sixth century BC. Teheran Archaeological Museum. (Photo Giraudon) D. G. Shepherd, 'An Achaemenid Sculpture in Lapis Lazuli', *The Bulletin of the Cleveland Museum of Art*, 48, 2, 1961.

76 Façade of the rock-cut tomb of Darius, Naqsh-i Rustam Valley, near Persepolis, Iran. (Photo Perissinotto) (5)

Index